Devotional Retreats

Biblical meditation
to open the heart and
rekindle the spirit

Debbonnaire Kovacs

Pacific Press® Publishing Association
Nampa, Idaho
Oshawa, Ontario, Canada

Edited by B. Russell Holt
Designed by Michelle C. Petz
Cover photos:(forest) © 2000 (Jeremy Walker/Stone)
(girl) © 2000 (Elke Selzle/Stone)

All Bible quotations not credited otherwise are from the New American Standard Bible, 1973.

Library of Congress Cataloging-in-Publication Data

Kovacs, Debbonnaire, 1954-
    Devotional retreats : biblical meditation to open the heart and
rekindle the spirit / Debbonnaire Kovacs.
        p. cm.
    ISBN 0-8163-1837-9
    1. Meditation—Christianity. 2. Bible—Devotional use. I. Title.

BS680.M38 K68 2001
248.3'4—dc21   00-066569

01 02 03 04 05 • 5 4 3 2 1

Contents

A Vision Quest

Meditation. How can one word have such myriad and diverse connotations? To some it means five minutes of relaxation a day, while to others it conjures up a picture of a gaunt ascetic walking unharmed through fire. What is meditation, anyway? Does relaxing your body and closing your eyes qualify? Or does it have to be an occult, bizarre, out-of-body experience?

More than twenty years ago, I decided to check it out. I had heard so much about all the possible benefits of meditation. I looked into some of the various meditation disciplines, such as Zen Buddhism, Yoga, and Transcendental Meditation. From my reading it appeared to me that for most devotees of these methods, the goal was to stop thinking entirely, vacate their minds, so that they could eventually reach nirvana (eternal unconsciousness), or open up to the Cosmic Awareness or whatever they perceived to be the ultimate human goal.

Physically, the complete relaxation that was required worked wonders, according to those who had tried it. The body grew stronger, more energetic, more youthful, and much more stress-resistant. That sounded great to me, but I really didn't think the mental emptiness was what I was looking for. It would be bad enough if emptiness was

5

all I got. But Jesus warned that an evil spirit who finds a mind empty, " 'swept, and put in order,' " will move in with seven of his buddies " 'more wicked than itself ' " (Matthew 12:44, 45).

Then it occurred to me that perhaps there was a way to combine the physical relaxation with Christian meditation—the kind of meditation that concentrates on something instead of nothing, the kind David meant when he said that a godly person meditates on God's law day and night (see Psalm 1:2).

So I tried it. And it worked! I received the physical and mental benefits as well as a much-strengthened awareness of God and His presence in my daily life. The relaxation techniques cleared my mind and helped my concentration, making it possible for my imagination to work much more vividly and realistically. In my mind, I could actually "see" and talk face-to-face with Jesus any time I wanted to! You can imagine what happened to the old "my-prayers-don't-get-past-the-ceiling" syndrome. He was never on the other side of the ceiling; He was right beside me all along. But obviously, I could not be as blessed by His presence as He wanted me to be if I was not aware of it. Becoming aware and appreciative of Jesus' continuous , loving attendance through the Holy Spirit opened up whole, astonishing new worlds to me—worlds of which no human has ever had more than glimpses. But, oh, what glorious glimpses! How they shone in my dreary world and made a rocky path better than a garden of roses! It was then, in the early 1980s, that I first wrote the main text of this book. I was so excited and longed so much to share my discoveries with other Christians everywhere. As I wrote, I felt the Holy Spirit hovering over me strongly, and I wrote it all in just a few weeks.

Looking back now, I suppose what happened next was inevitable. With 20/20 hindsight, I can simplify a very long, very tangled path by saying that there were two major events. One was a videotape in which a man said that all meditation was evil and of the devil, an occult attempt to "conjure up" the Lord and get Him to do what you want. He quoted selections from Ellen White's writings to back up his conclusion. The effect this had on me was interesting, to say the least. I could clearly see that the man was an expert at manipulating his audience by speech, mannerism, and body language. I knew that the Bible tells us to meditate; so does Ellen White. And I knew that I certainly was not "conjuring up" the Jesus who promised to be with me always and to teach and guide me in the way I should go. More than that, when I looked up the passages this man had quoted from Ellen White's writings, I found he had left out some very pertinent parts.

Yet he frightened me. What if he was even a little bit right? What if I *was* misleading myself and putting words into the mouth of God? Nothing, it seemed to me, could be more blasphemous than that! Worse yet, what if I succeeded in publishing my book and misled others as well? I turned where I always turn—to God. But there was now an insidious doubt. How could He answer me? What if it wasn't Him? I studied the Bible. I found what I had always found, but now I doubted my own ability to understand what I read. What if I was interpreting Scripture to suit myself? How would I know? I asked others. But I didn't know whether they were right either. If God couldn't answer me, how could anyone else?

Then the second event happened. In a serious crisis in my life, I had a season of prayerful meditation, which was so real and so personal that to this day I feel as if I could almost have tape-recorded the voice of God. Not really, of course, but that's how it felt. As one who has known and loved Jesus from my earliest babyhood, I knew it was Him. I still know it was Him. And He said some astonishing things.

Only some of which came true.

You can only imagine my growing desperation as the traumatic years followed each other, and I waited and waited. The thing for which I had been waiting—the thing I thought Jesus had promised me—never happened.

If I could tell you my anguish! Perhaps you've been there. What now? There was no question of turning against God. I knew He was there and that He loved me and that He had good plans for me, as well—better!—than I knew my own name. But how could He guide me? How could I ever dare to listen to Him again?

As time passed and my perspective came somewhat more into focus, I was able to accept that the thing for which I had longed had not happened; I was able to go on without it. It was no longer the issue. Yet my mind kept going back feverishly, again and again, to that same event. I felt I *had* to understand. The issue was God's ability to lead me. How could He even tell me what I had done wrong or help me to do better if I could not hear Him? It was an impasse. I could see no way around it.

"Lord," I said, "You will have to lead me by providence, by opening and shutting doors, by putting a ring in my nose if You have to! I want only Your will, but I no longer know how to find it unless it's something obvious. I want to listen to You. I will again, if You can show me how. Only You can answer this burning question. I don't see how You can do it and make me *know* it's You, but I hope You can. I'll wait and see."

And for years, that's where I was stuck. This manuscript, and my devotional life, sat on the shelf. I still studied; I still prayed; I was still active in church; I still grew in many ways. I never for a moment lost my faith that God would ultimately prevail, but I simply could not see how. I thought perhaps I would have my question answered only in heaven.

But, oh, how I missed Him! I tried, occasionally, to talk with Him as I used to, but I was too afraid, and so I would cry myself to sleep.

But Jesus, patient Jesus, knew what to do and took His time. Little by little, He calmed my fears and taught me to trust Him again. The end of this story is like its beginning—a long, tangled path marked by a few events I can put my finger on.

Like one of the few times He succeeded in coming to me as He used to.

He took me into the garden in my heart where we used to walk and talk together and showed me something that shocked me. In the center of that garden, I imagine a tree, which represents the tree of my life. The spring bubbling up at its roots represents the Holy Spirit, the ever-living spring Jesus promised in John 4 to those who believe on Him. The spring, not to my surprise, was muddy and full of leaves, but that wasn't what Jesus wanted to show me. He pulled back some weeds and showed me a dark cavern at the roots of the tree. Wrapped around the roots, sucking out their life, twisting and distorting their growth, was the biggest, ugliest, most terrifying serpent I had ever imagined.

"It's Fear," said Jesus. "You've let it take over your life, and it will kill you in time. May I get rid of it?"

"Please!" I wept and hid my eyes while He wrestled the thing, hissing and screaming, from its lair and flung it into outer darkness. But the roots were now so thin and weak and twisted that I didn't know if they could ever be as strong as they once were.

"It takes time," said Jesus. "Let's clean out this spring."

It took time, all right. Years.

Finally, in the late 1990s, things started to come unstuck. That was when, in a small group at camp meeting, I shared just a touch of my fear and the fact that my writing, which I knew God wanted me to do, was stuck with everything else. "How do I dare to tell people anything about God?" I demanded. "I don't know anything!"

"Maybe," said a quiet young man I'll never forget, "that's what God has been waiting for."

It stopped me cold. Could it be? That day, I said, "I'll write, Lord." And only after I said that did it dawn on me that this is one of the ways God does talk to me and makes me know it's Him. Believe me, when I write, insights come up on my computer screen that I know are not from me!

The minute I said I'd write, doors began to open. It was awesome. This manuscript began to nag at the back of my mind more and more, as New Age concepts grew stronger and it became ever more vital that Christians understand clearly what God means by meditation and what the devil means. But my question still remained. What could I say? So I left it on the shelf.

Then came camp meeting 1999. One of the lessons, as always, was trusting God. Do you know, He's bigger than the devil? No, I mean, do you *know?*

The last day of camp meeting I went to the bookstore. I knew what I wanted to buy there, but I didn't buy it. To my surprise, instead, I bought Morris Venden's *How to Know God's Will in Your Life.* I read it in three afternoons the next week. In that book, which I cannot recommend highly enough, Elder Venden lists eight ways to know the will of God. Mind you, they are nothing new. He says he got seven of them from George Mueller. Any Christian would recognize them. At first, as I read, I was muttering, "I know that! I *know* that!" But in every chapter he said, over and over again (for hard-headed types like me), "You have to follow all eight together! No one thing, not even Bible study or prayer, is safe by itself. You can honestly get off the track if you don't follow all eight together!" Or words to that effect.

And the doors flew open. They just flew open! The answer to my question—Is it, or is it not, safe to prayerfully imagine conversations with God—is Yes, it is safe, as *one part of a whole, well-rounded Christian understanding of how God leads us!* I had gotten off the track by overemphasizing one subjective experience, rather than balancing it with prayer, study, good counsel, providence, and so on. And from that point, I just plain got scared and lost all perspective. For the first time, everything was clear, and I knew it wasn't Morris Venden or George Mueller or any other human who had made it so. It was God. It was my Friend. I *knew* it.

There are no words to express my joy and relief. I filled pages of my journal with stars and exclamation points and underlines. I cried. I told my friends and family. Most of all, I thanked God. I went back to meditation. I hugged Jesus and cried some more. This is one of the few times I can honestly say I wouldn't choose to have been led a different way. Looking back, I can see that every step was necessary in order that I could have the absolute certainty that I have today. My assurance can never be shaken again that when Jesus said, "Your ears will hear a word behind you, 'This is the way, walk in it,' whenever you turn to the right or to the left" (Isaiah 30:21), that's exactly what He meant. In other words, if we will be certain to follow Him in *all* His ways, He'll get us back on track whenever we stray (as we sometimes will).

Then I got this manuscript off the shelf. Now I knew what to say.

2

Meditation 101

So, we're back to our original question: Just what is meditation, and how does Christian meditation differ from the world's counterfeit? The Bible's answer may surprise you. It certainly surprised me.

The English word "meditate" is listed fourteen times in my *Strong's Concordance*, only two times in the New Testament, and one of those—Luke 21:14—really should say "premeditate." "Meditation" is listed six times, all of them in the Old Testament. Fifteen of these references are in the Psalms, and seven of those are in Psalm 119. Interestingly, Psalm 119 uses a different Hebrew word than the other passages use. It is *siyach*, which means, and I quote Strong exactly, "to *ponder*, i.e. (by impl.) *converse* (with oneself, and hence aloud) or (trans.) *utter:*—commune, complain, declare, meditate, muse, pray, speak, talk (with)." Other than Psalm 119, only Psalm 104:34 uses the noun form of this word.

The rest of the Old Testament passages in which "meditate" occurs use forms of another Hebrew word—*hagah*—which means, again I quote, "to *murmur* (in pleasure or anger); by impl. to *ponder:*—imagine, meditate, mourn, mutter . . . ." So the two Hebrew words are pretty much equal in meaning. It was at this point that I began to think how strange it was that the Hebrew words for "meditate" seem to include so much sound. I knew from my earlier reading that non-Christian forms of meditation often included sounds. A bell rang in my mind. What was that text about "wizards that peep and mutter"?

I looked it up. It's in Isaiah 8:19. Here it is, from the New American Standard Bible: "And when they say to you, 'Consult the mediums and the spiritists who whisper and mutter,' should not a people consult their God?" I looked in the lexicon to find out what word was translated "mutter." Imagine my astonishment to discover it is *hagah*—same word, same form, same tense as " 'This book of the law shall not depart from your mouth, but you shall *meditate* on it day and night' " (Joshua 1:8, italics supplied)—a direct command to Joshua from God. The same word as "in His law he *meditates* day and night" (Psalm 1:2, italics supplied). The same word as "I *meditate* on Thee in the night watches" (Psalm 63:6, italics supplied) and many more! I was shocked. Clearly, the *action* the wizards were performing was not wrong—in fact, we are commanded to do it. What then made them wrong? Let's go back to Isaiah 8.

"*Should they consult* the dead on behalf of the living? To the law and to the testimony! If they do not speak according to this word, it is because they have no dawn" (verses 19, 20). ["No light in them" KJV.] These wizards and mediums are using a God-given form of communication to consult, not the dead, of course, but the devil. They are then using the information they receive to lead the people who believe in them away from the Word of God. The Lord makes it very clear what He thinks of these practices in the following verses. Here is His strongly worded warning:

"And they will pass through the land hard-pressed and famished, and it will turn out that when they are hungry, they will be enraged and curse their king and their God as they face upward. Then they will look to the earth, and behold, distress and darkness, the gloom of anguish; and *they will be* driven away into darkness" (verses 21, 22).

But what about those who do not follow these deceivers? "But there will be no *more* gloom for her who was in anguish; . . . The people who walk in darkness will see a great light" (Isaiah 9:1, 2). And there follows one of the most beautiful of Messianic prophecies.

Is any of this still going on in this enlightened age? Of course. We know it today by the charming, if inaccurate, name of the "New Age." The principle is crystal clear. Meditation connects you with somebody. You might want to be certain with whom you are connecting! This was one of the things that used to scare me back when I was letting fear rule. But now I have been reminded in ways I can never forget that God is bigger than Satan and will never allow His children to be snatched from His hand (see John 10:28). Every one of the above texts makes it clear that we are to meditate upon God, His law (the "Book of the Law," that is, the Bible), and His works. To be afraid to do that is like being afraid to use the telephone in case you might get a wrong number. "Draw near to God and He will draw near to you" (James 4:8). It's a promise.

Here, then, is the method that works for me. Try it, experiment with it, pray about it, change it. Do whatever it takes to make it a tool for you—a tool that will bring you closer to the One who loves you best of all.

Step One: Pray

There is no Christian meditation without prayer, no matter how pure may be the motives of the person attempting the meditating. In fact, in a way it's misleading to call prayer a "step," since Christian meditation *is* prayer. Begin by asking God to help you relax, stop worrying, and put down your burdens. He'll tell you, " 'My peace I give to you; . . . Let not your heart be troubled, nor let it be fearful' " (John

14:27). Ask Him to forgive your sins and take away your own desires and wishes that might confuse you. He'll remind you, "Trust in [Me] with all your heart, and do not lean on your own understanding. In all your ways acknowledge [Me], and [I] will make your paths straight" (see Proverbs 3:5, 6). Ask the Holy Spirit to come into your mind and help you to gain exactly what you need from this time with Him. And hear Jesus answer, " 'The Helper, the Holy Spirit, whom the Father will send in My name, He will teach you all things, and bring to your remembrance all that I said to you' " (John 14:26).

Step Two: Prepare

We will be examining and practicing two different types of meditation—scriptural and personal. Personal meditation—private talks between you and your Master—will be discussed at more length in a later chapter. The majority of this book will concentrate on scriptural meditation.

The primary key to scriptural meditation—your Bible—is implicit in its name. You must choose and carefully read a passage upon which to meditate. Choose—there's the rub! The Word of God is packed so full of gems with personal treasures for you, His beloved child, that choosing just one is sometimes a difficult task in itself. If you have a specific need or problem, your choice is easier. Use a concordance or one of those lists of passages addressing a variety of needs, moods, or problems contained in the back of many Bibles.

If you just want to feel close to Him (what could be more important, after all?) pick a story from His life or choose a favorite Bible story with which you are already familiar. You'll be surprised what new things you'll learn!

In a pinch, you can just open the Bible and point. Unless you hit the genealogies (and maybe even then), I can almost guarantee you'll find a vivid picture of God.

Here's an important note if you have never done anything like this and are afraid you haven't enough imagination. This book is for you, with love. I hope it will start you on your way to an exciting and valuable experience, because I believe with all my heart that God gave you just the mind you need in order to know Him. Of course, He also expects you to develop ever-increasing abilities to see and hear Him, and it won't always be easy. Sometimes it will seem impossible. But He said you could know Him, and " 'has He spoken, and will He not make it good?' " (Numbers 23:19). Of course He will! Before He would fail, the stars would fall right down from the sky.

And here's a encouraging note from someone else, too. Ellen White was speaking to someone who had not accepted truth that was new to him, so she uses "if-you-had,-God-would-have" language. That means that for someone who wants to accept all the truth God has, it could also read "if you do, God will." Here is what she says: "If you had received the truth into a good and honest heart, you would have become a living channel of light, with clear perception and sanctified imagination. Your conceptions of truth would have been exalted, and your heart made joyful in God. God would have given you a testimony clear, powerful, and convincing" (*Ellen G. White 1888 Materials*, p. 1052).

As you read, please keep your Bible near at hand. Each meditation will begin by listing a scriptural passage or passages, and the depth of the blessing you receive will be dependent on how much care you take to become familiar with God's Word before going on. What the Bible says is far more important than anything I say, or anything you think, *about* the Bible.

You will especially need your Bible after your meditation if you feel that God has given you any new or different understanding about truth. Check what you think He told you with what He has already said. Remember what we read in Isaiah 8:20: "If they do not speak according to this word, it is because they have no dawn," or no light. It's possible to be honest and still get off track, if you don't immediately check your impressions with God's revealed Word. That's why Morris Venden keeps repeating, *all* those ways to know God's will must work together! We will deal with this aspect in more detail in chapter 16, when we study personal meditation.

Step Three: Relax

The thing you need most is often the hardest thing to come by—at least fifteen or twenty minutes of peace. The more you need meditation in your life, the harder it will be to obtain it. That's what "stress" means. But do what you have to—Jesus is patiently standing by, longing to talk with you.

Once you have a comfortable spot and some quiet time to yourself, you're ready to begin. Meditation can be done anywhere—a comfortable chair, the floor, even a tree branch outdoors is great if you can manage it. Just don't lie down; you'll go to sleep.

You have already asked the Lord to clear your mind of the cluttered, worried, and (let's face it) self-centered thoughts that usually live there. But you'll find it's not as easy as you wish to cooperate with Him. Your mind is so used to *scrambling,* on six levels, at ninety miles an hour, that it takes practice to shift into neutral. An almost universal complaint of beginners at meditation is, "I can't do it. My mind just wanders!" Remember, this is not a performance. No one is grading you on how perfectly or how quickly you can free your mind from turmoil. Don't get upset or impatient with yourself. Tense meditation is a contradiction in terms—it can't be done! Like everything else in the Christian life, we must pray for the faith to let go and let God do it for us.

Remember the old saying about "not thinking about the green-eyed monkey"? As soon as someone says that, what do you think of?

17

It's impossible to "not think" about anything. Remember our Bible study. Others may meditate on nothingness, but Christians must meditate on something—actually, on Someone. Fix Jesus' face in your mind's eye. Don't worry, He knows you don't know what He really looks like, and He doesn't mind how you imagine Him. Apparently in Bible times, people meditated out loud. So you could say, or murmur, or whisper one of the names of God. Or you could sing. It is well known that music goes to the heart as nothing else can do. The important thing is to think of something that will help you to concentrate on Him. Not on thoughts about Him or to Him or from Him, yet, but just on *Him*. When intruding thoughts come in, calmly and patiently turn your mind back to its focal point. "In the strength of God the imagination can be disciplined to dwell upon things which are pure and heavenly" (*Mind, Character, and Personality*), vol. II, p. 595.

One more point. I hate to bring this up (because it makes me feel guilty), but the healthfulness of your lifestyle has a bearing on your devotional life. Not only can a clear mind pray better, but it can listen and obey much better as well. But if you are not living as healthfully as you might, certainly don't let that stop you from meditating. How else will He enable you to overcome that appetite—or whatever the problem may be? Here's something you can do right now that will help to clear your mind even if the bloodstream is a little more sluggish than it ought to be. Take several deep breaths, (preferably outside or in front of an open window), inhaling from the abdomen, not from the chest. Exhale slowly and completely, to clean stale air out of your lungs and get your circulation going. Then with eyes closed, begin to breathe slowly and evenly, consciously relaxing your body, especially the muscles of the face, neck, and shoulders, where tension collects. Take God at His word when He says He'll grant you His peace; feel your tension, anger, depression, busyness, or whatever, all drain away.

Step Four: Be There

Now you're ready to use your senses to create the scene of your encounter with God in your mind. What can you see, hear, smell, feel, taste? What season is it? Where are you and what are you doing? Are you inside, outside, walking, or sitting?

"Let us in imagination go back to that scene, and, as we sit with the disciples on the mountainside, enter into the thoughts and feelings that filled their hearts. Understanding what the words of Jesus meant to those who heard them, we may discern in them a new vividness and beauty, and may also gather for ourselves their deeper lessons" (*Thoughts From the Mount of Blessing*, p. 1).

When the scene is real and you feel yourself "there," begin the action. Look up and see Jesus, or whatever scriptural scene you have chosen. Go through the story and be a part of it. Find out what it means to you. A good description of this process is found in *Desire of Ages*, page 83. "It would be well for us to spend a thoughtful hour each day in contemplation of the life of Christ. We should take it point by point, and let the imagination grasp each scene, especially the closing ones. As we thus dwell upon His great sacrifice for us, our confidence in Him will be more constant, our love will be quickened, and we shall be more deeply imbued with His spirit."

Step Five: Come Back

Close with another prayer. Thank Jesus for being with you and for what you have learned from Him. Then open your eyes, breathe deeply, stretch, and get up slowly. And then, *don't* imagine yourself saying goodbye to Jesus and going about your business. That's the difference between this kind of meditation and the pale copies. When a busy executive merely takes five minutes to relax, her body benefits. When she gets up, she picks up her burdens again, feeling more able to cope with the stresses of her complex life. But we *leave* our burdens. We put them in hands that know much more than we do about how to take care of them, and we leave them there. We get up and take Him with us to do the dishes or to guide our hands as we fix a car or mend a broken body. Wherever you go, whatever you do, your best Friend wants to go and do it with you.

3

He Looks for Me

A great deal has been said and written about humanity's search for God, but the truth is that nobody would ever look for God in the first place if God did not start looking first. The Trinity is so continuously engrossed in finding ways into human hearts that the only way *not* to find God is to spend every moment of one's life busily and determinedly working at not finding Him. And it *is* work. Ask Saul of Tarsus. Ask the woman at the well. For that matter, ask yourself.

God says in His Word that He is not willing to lose any of us (see 2 Peter 3:9). If you've been a Christian very long, you already know that when God is unwilling that something should happen, it is, by definition, a monumental task to talk Him into letting it happen. He still won't be willing. But He is even less willing to enslave a child of His heart. So, with tears on His face, He watches many turn their backs, run away, and refuse to let Him find them.

Yes, it is possible. But it is hard.

Ask Judas.

Finding God, on the other hand, is the easiest thing in the world. Just turn around, and you'll find Him there—with arms outstretched and joy in His loving eyes. He'll welcome you and cry out to anyone who will listen, " ' "Rejoice with me, for I have found my sheep!" ' " (Luke 15:6).

He is the One who stays out all night, searching. Funny creatures that we humans are, it surprises us every time.

Our first scriptural meditation details one man's wonder when he discovered that before he even knew Jesus existed, the Master had His eyes on him. In preparation, please read John 1:43-51. Read these verses through several times, paying close attention to the dialogue, so that you will be clear on the details in your own mind.

Background

In order to do full justice to a scriptural meditation, it is necessary to know the context of the story. This incident takes place at the very beginning of Christ's ministry. He is just beginning to gather together that faithful dozen who will travel with Him, work with Him, argue with Him, love Him, and be trained and prayed over by Him so that they—all save one—may carry on His work when He has gone.

It is early spring—almost time for Passover (see John 2:13).

A note on "role-playing." Let's look again at what Ellen White says in *Thoughts From the Mount of Blessing.* "Let us in imagination go back to that scene, and, as we sit with the disciples on the mountainside, enter into the thoughts and feelings that filled their hearts. Understanding what the words of Jesus meant to those who heard them, we may discern in them a new vividness and beauty, and may also gather for ourselves their deeper lessons" (p. 1). I see this as suggesting two possible directions to take in any scriptural meditation. We may, by "entering into the thoughts and feelings" of the characters, try to understand what *they* were thinking. In other words, I can pretend to be Peter or whoever may figure in the story. Or we may pretend we ourselves are there, trying to imagine what *we* would have thought and felt if these things had hap-

22

pened to us, and "gather for ourselves their deeper meanings." It can be very enriching to do both and even to try on the roles of different characters in the same story. You will often gain a different blessing each time. In this particular example, we are going to play the role of Nathanael.

Recreate the scene in your own mind, imagining what it might have been like if you were Nathanael. Use all five senses. What is the weather like? Sunny and mild, or perhaps a little warmer, as befits a desert country?

You are sitting under a fig tree. Are you sitting on the ground? On a chair? On a stone?

What can you feel? The rough bark of the tree against your back? The breeze lifting your hair? The leaf-filtered warmth of sunshine?

What do you smell? Is there bread baking in a nearby oven? Are flowers blooming? Can you smell the dusty street and your own home-spun wool garments?

What do you hear? Are birds singing, dogs barking? Perhaps a donkey clip-clops by, pulling a creaking wagon, or a mother calls to her child. Maybe children are laughing and shouting.

What do you see? I picture a squat little town with whitewashed houses eye-dazzling in the sunshine, fig trees, vineyards, and miniature herb gardens at kitchen doors. I can see bright-robed, bearded men and dark-eyed, veiled women going about their business. I see bare-legged children running down the street and a baking mother keeping a careful eye on her toddler. Imagine a contemptuous, stern-faced Roman soldier riding down the street and see the fear mixed with resentment in the eyes of the Jews who scuttle nervously out of his way.

Last of all, how are you feeling? Are you happy, sad, tired, contented? Make it real for you. Be there.

Now look around and see your good friend Philip racing toward you, bursting with exciting news of some kind. Maybe you get up and go to meet him.

As soon as he is near enough, Philip exclaims without preamble, " 'We have found Him of whom Moses in the Law and *also* the Prophets wrote, Jesus of Nazareth, the son of Joseph' " (John 1:45).

What a bombshell! You are a Jew, born and bred, and you know exactly of whom Philip speaks. The Messiah Himself! What are your feelings? Astonishment? Joy? Perhaps just a little healthy skepticism? For centuries your people have waited and prayed for their Deliverer. Lately there has been an epidemic of pretenders to the title, most of whom have been quickly squashed by Rome, followers and all. Is it possible that the real Messiah has appeared now—today—and in Nazareth, of all unlikely places? Still, you know Philip well, and he surely would not make a sweeping statement like that out of thin air.

From all the whirling melee of questions in your mind, only the least important and most ridiculous one blurts itself out in words: " 'Can any good thing come out of Nazareth?' "

Philip makes no attempt to convince or compel. He merely says, " 'Come and see' " (verse 46).

So you go.

As you walk, Philip tells you about his brief knowledge of Jesus. From the way he talks, you may be surprised when you actually see the object of all this commotion. He is, after all, only a young and humbly dressed Galilean. But as you near Him, He stops talking and looks up; suddenly you meet His compelling gaze. Picture Him in your mind as you think He really looked.

Don't miss the vital significance of this contact—even though Nathanael probably did, at least until later. This is the most important moment of any meditation. You are standing in a dusty village street in Israel, face to face with the Creator of that very dust and of the eyes through which you see Him, the air you breathe, the sun above you.

And He looks at you with joy and says, " 'Behold, an Israelite indeed, in whom is no guile!' " (verse 47).

Now how do you feel? A compliment like that from the Lord of the universe!

In your role as Nathanael, you stare in astonishment and ask, " 'How do You know me?' "

Jesus smiles. " 'Before Philip called you, when you were under the fig tree, I saw you' " (verse 48).

And there you have it. Jesus has been looking for you. Yes, *you*— not just Nathanael. What is your reaction to that? Are you elated, frightened, uneasy? May you cry out with joy, as Nathanael did, " 'Rabbi, You are the Son of God; You are the King of Israel!' " (verse 49).

He has been watching over you, looking for you, longing to have you turn to Him. Jesus would spend the last ounce of His infinite energy and patience looking for you, if it were necessary, and count it all well lost if He could find you and have you say, "You are the Son of God and my King!"

His response would be the same to you as it was to the exuberant Nathanael. His smile would widen, and He would say, "You shall see much greater things than these, My precious child."

So keep your eyes open. He always means what He says. And the first great thing He wants to do, the moment He finds you, is start to fix whatever is wrong. It doesn't matter what it is—how big or small it is or how many problems you have—if there's anything hurting you, your Jesus wants to heal it.

4

He Heals Me

The rest of the meditations in this book, instead of leading you through the stories with questions and suggestions, are written as I imagine them. I offer them to you only as guides. The reason this book exists is that you and I may better learn to hear God speaking to us individually. So don't just read these meditations my way. Go back and experience them your way. Or choose other portions of Scripture that are especially meaningful to you.

The story in this chapter is one that means a great deal to me. It is the story of a paralytic man Jesus healed, and although I have never been physically paralyzed, I do know how it feels to be mentally and emotion-ally paralyzed with my whole life stuck in a rut from which there seems to be no escape. Have you ever felt that way? Then come with me on a journey through healing. In preparation, read all three versions of this story—Matthew 9:1-7; Mark 2:1-12; and Luke 5:17-26.

Background

The place is Capernaum, Jesus' "own town" where Jesus has settled after His cousin, John the Baptist, was taken into custody (see Mat-thew 4:13). Jesus has been preaching for some time now, and His reputation and the multitudes, both those who love Him and those who hate Him, are growing.

I don't know the season. I imagine it as a hot, sunny day. Jesus' house is filled to the brim with listeners, including Pharisees and teachers from all over Israel. It is so crowded that the friends who carry the paralytic to Jesus cannot get through. Being determined, they resort to unusual tactics to gain admittance. We join them on the roof.

* * *

It seems to take forever for them to make a hole big enough for my pallet to go through. As the hole enlarges, the sounds from inside the house grow clearer—murmuring, shuffling crowd sounds, a baby's whimper, quickly shushed, and above it all, His voice. In that voice, calm quiet blends with authority and assurance, and I feel I could listen forever, but it stops suddenly.

There is a moment of silence, and then a rush of indistinguishable noise from the crowd, and I realize we have been discovered. My heart pounds painfully as my friends manage to secure the rope in such a way that it will lift and hold me in my pallet.

Slowly, slowly I am lowered through the roof to hang suspended right in the middle of the room before the Rabbi and all those astonished people. Their questions and exclamations rise around me like a wave, and I'm flushed with embarrassment and apprehension. Then Jesus makes a slight gesture, and silence falls again.

I think this is even worse—dangling here in this breathless hush, swaying a little on the ends of my ropes. I am sure everyone in the room can hear my heart beating. After a stifling eternity of a moment, I dare to lift my eyes to meet His. And in that moment, the room and everyone in it disappears.

Those eyes! They burn through me like blue fire, comfort me like a mother's touch, embrace me like a lover. My pain, embarrassment, and fear are gone. He sees me, knows me, and He loves me anyway!

It must seem obvious to everyone that I have come here desperate for physical healing—I thought so myself. But Jesus knows my real burden, the one I have not dared hope that even He might lift.

" 'My son, your sins are forgiven' " (Mark 2:5).

Joy floods me and overflows in tears. I am content. What matters now a life burdened with dead limbs? I have survived with them for a long time and am willing now to continue to do so, for my soul lives!

But there is a stir, and the packed room intrudes on my consciousness again. Jesus looks beyond me, sorrow and sternness in His eyes. For the first time, I look around me. My eyes fall upon a group of scribes, whispering angrily together and sending dagger glances both at me and the Man who has saved me.

Jesus is speaking again, and I watch the scribes, haughty and disdainful in their rich robes. " 'Why are you reasoning about these things in your hearts? Which is easier, to say to the paralytic, "Your sins are forgiven"; or to say, "Arise, and take up your pallet and walk"?' " (verses 8, 9).

The scribes deign to give no answer. Their intention to disagree with anything He says is obvious in their glowering faces. But at the Master's next words, my attention flies from the scribes as if they were never there, and I turn my head with a gasp to watch His face again. " 'But in order that you may know that the Son of Man has authority on earth to forgive sins,' "—He looks at me, and the sadness leaves His eyes— " 'I say to you, rise, take up your pallet and go home' " (verses 10, 11).

In terror, I close my eyes. I thought I was content only to be forgiven. I felt quite noble about it. Now I find that, actually, I was relieved. I am afraid to be healed! I want it more than anything. But— walk! How can He say it so casually? He is not paralyzed. He doesn't know.

I have heard He can do these things, but I *feel* no different. My body is as leaden as ever. What if the scoffers are right? How can this ordinary-looking man have such God-like powers? A whirlwind of agonizing thought passes in an instant before I open my eyes to meet His again.

Then a strange thing happens. I find I can't look into those calm, encouraging eyes and not believe every single word He may choose to say, no matter how strange and impossible it seems to me.

So, clinging resolutely to those eyes, I lift my hand.

And it works! My hand moves! My heart pounds; my whole body fills with a warm, tingling feeling. My head is positively giddy with elation and relief and wonder and a million other emotions as (nearly tipping out of the swinging pallet in my excitement) I actually make it to my feet!

Jesus' smile surpasses my own in joy as He reaches out to give me a hand. His eyes shine as if He loves to heal me more than I love to be whole.

My first coherent thought, after I try to stumble out my gratitude, is of my family. They must see me! They must know! They must come back and meet this Man!

Trembling, I gather up my mat and rush home, singing God's praises at the top of my voice, and leaving my friends to excitedly patch up the hole and follow.

* * *

I'd like to share with you an example of how personally meaningful this kind of meditation can be. While reading back over these pages, looking for meanings for myself, I discovered a phrase whose hidden significance for me is astonishing. "He is not paralyzed. He doesn't know."

It so happens that I once wrote in my journal, "Were You ever depressed? I mean really depressed? Did You ever get sick and tired of the everlasting press of the selfish multitude and the impregnable stupidity of Your disciples? I find it hard to believe. That's why I feel so evil admitting to my feelings of hostility and anger even toward my own family."

If you and I are using this man's paralysis as a figure for our own—sometimes staggering—spiritual paralysis, then the issue is the same. Does He really know what it is like to be you? We know He was tempted as we are, yet without sin (Hebrews 4:15). How did that work? I don't know. I don't think even the angels know. It's one of those mysteries for which we'll never grow tired of praising Him. All you and I need to know is that He said He can heal us and told us how to get that healing.

Is your heart weary and perplexed, in sore need of a healing hand? Do you feel paralyzed and useless, as if you're just so much dead weight littering up life's highway? Come to Jesus now, this minute. You don't even need enterprising friends to make an entrance into His presence. He's right beside you and has been all along.

Your solution is the same one the paralytic found. If your Lord says you can step out of your anger, depression, and hopelessness, then fix your eyes on His through prayer and meditation, cling to His hand through claiming His promises and His unshakable faith as your own, and step out! A moment is all it takes, and you're His—and safe so long as you stay under His wings. Bear in mind that staying under His wings includes doing whatever He asks you to do next, and that may include seeking professional help, as well.

Healing! There's nothing like it. No words can ever convey the excitement and release of the real thing. And He does dearly love to do it. He pleads with us through every means at His disposal to let Him come into us and make us forever whole.

5

He Intercedes for Me

All Jesus needed to know at any given point in His life was "What is My Father's will?" The night He faced His last Passover—the real Passover, the one all the others had foreshadowed—was no exception. In Jesus' divinity, when it came to a choice between Himself and you, there was simply no contest.

In His human side, however, there was a contest such as the universe has never seen before or since. The only thing that held Him through this most difficult night of His life was the law, that transcript of His own character—He loved His Father and He loved you (see Matthew 22:37-40). Just thinking of you was one of the things that gave Him the strength to go on. How do I know this? It's in John 17:20, 21.

The meditation in this chapter will concentrate on Jesus' Gethsemane ordeal. In preparation, please read His intercessory prayer for you and me in John 17, as well as the three Gethsemane accounts—Matthew 26:36-46; Mark 14:32-42; and Luke 22:39-46.

Background

It is spring A.D. 31—the darkest spring in the annals of the earth, and Jesus and His disciples have just finished eating Passover together for the last time. The disciples have argued as usual, and Jesus has given them a graphic example of what He means when He says "love" by washing their feet. Judas's intentions have been uncovered, and he has gone into the night.

Jesus has spent the rest of the evening trying to explain Himself and His mission more clearly than ever to these overgrown children of His, who are so soon going to have to carry on the work He has begun. He gives some of His most precious messages to them at this time, and only the beloved John appears to have been listening closely enough to write it all down later (see John 14; 15; 16). Let us go now with our Lord and His eleven remaining disciples to Gethsemane, and although we almost certainly would not have done so had we been there, let's stay awake!

An important note before we begin: The disciples did not fall asleep out of simple, selfish carelessness. The devil had two aims in making them feel such a heavy sleepiness that they nodded off in spite of their best efforts. One was so that Jesus would have no human support and, consequently, would be easier to beat. The other was so that the disciples would miss out on the tremendous blessing they could have gained from helping the One who had always helped them to go through the darkest hour of His life.

Satan has the same goal concerning you and me. It may be difficult at first to get much out of this story. The accounts are necessarily terse—the reporters were asleep. But Jesus remembers that night very well indeed, and He is willing to help us learn from it whatever we most need to know. The disciples could have stayed awake through God's power only, and that is also what we shall need for this meditation.

He Intercedes for Me

*   *   *

It is late, and getting chilly as we walk toward the Garden. A few birds still twitter momentarily, and occasionally some small night creature scurries away from our footsteps, but for the most part everything sleeps and the Garden is still.

I imagine it as a dark, cloudy night with only an occasional star twinkling through the blackness and perhaps a here-and-gone-again moon. We pull our woolen mantles about us and shiver, not entirely from the cold. There is something unnerving in the air tonight. It is almost as if some danger is at hand, and yet Jesus seems in no hurry to escape anywhere, or even to arm Himself and be prepared for trouble. But then, how many times has He sighed at our lack of faith? This is God's chosen One! We are more assured of it than ever. God will certainly not allow anything to happen to Him. Anyway, we are as one in our determination to defend Him with our lives if necessary.

Still, we cannot help stealing worried looks at His face. We have been with Him through everything these last few years, and never— not at Lazarus's death, not even when His cousin John was executed— have we seen Him look like this. If only we could *do* something!

As we enter the Garden, the darkness seems suddenly more oppressive than ever. Only an occasional moonbeam makes it through the branches of the gnarled old trees and vines. I can smell the dampness of dirt and old stones.

Jesus turns to us. " 'Sit here while I go over there and pray' " (Matthew 26:36).

We are relieved and readily find places to sit or lie down. Prayer! That's what He needs! We've seen it before. Whenever Jesus is troubled, He goes off alone to pray, and when He returns, He is the calm, assured Master we know and love. We need not fear now.

Jesus motions to His three closest friends—Peter, James, and John—

to follow Him. I, too, steal nearer to His side. He is becoming more and more deeply grieved and distressed. His very steps seem difficult, and His voice sounds labored as He says, " 'My soul is deeply grieved, to the point of death; remain here and keep watch with Me' " (verse 38).

"Keep watch," I think I hear Peter murmur. "Now that's more like it!" And with one hand on his sword, he finds a place with his back to Jesus, where he has a vantage point over the Garden.

But I stare at Jesus, feeling frightened. I'd be rich if I had a nickel for every time I've said, "I think I'm going to die!" But Jesus isn't exaggerating. He staggers on a little farther and falls to the ground as though the weight of the world is on His back.

And so it begins. Everywhere else on this planet people must be having a peculiarly peaceful, temptationless time as Satan bends all the evil forces of his legions on this one young Galilean. For Satan knows, as the drowsy disciples do not, that on the outcome of this contest hangs the fate of all God's sovereignty, not only for this world, but throughout the universe. If he can win this battle, then his lies about God become truth, and he wins the war.

Yet as the Son's life on earth began, so it comes to its climax, and so it will end, with all of heaven holding its collective breath in agony, all the watching worlds gasping with horror and awe, and with the earth— the only reason for Jesus' heartbreak and heaven's loss—sleeping in indifferent silence.

" 'Abba!' " I hear His tears of anguish. " 'Father! All things are possible for Thee; remove this cup from Me; yet not what I will, but what Thou wilt' " (Mark 14:36).

And that is as far as our reporters made it before their heavy eyelids closed, so we do not know with what words God's only Son continued to pour out His sorrow to His Father. But we have the key to His temptations in this one line.

He Intercedes for Me

We hear a great deal about Jesus' agonizing decision to go on rather than to quit and leave us as we deserve to be left. And surely that was part of it. It goes without saying that Satan pulled out all the stops and tried any temptation that occurred to him.

But he also knew this Man. Jesus had a perfect record for choosing obedience to God over disobedience. It is not likely (to me) that that temptation carried much more weight with Him than it ever did. But if Satan could get Him to believe that there might be *some other way* of fulfilling God's will—now that's temptation!

"Father, with Thee all things are possible." Who knows that better than Jesus? "If only there is some other way!" He longs for that—who wouldn't? But there is no other way. He knows that too. And if it is a choice between obeying and disobeying, if it is a choice between heaven and you—His darling child—Jesus makes the choice He has always made without a pause. "Not My will, but Thine."

A little of the agony lifts, and Jesus, longing for the arms of His friends, staggers to where He left them. They awaken, startled and guilty, staring at His tortured face.

"Peter, are you asleep? Could you not watch one hour?" Hear the pain and disappointment in His weakened voice. But for whom is His concern, even now? " 'Keep watching and praying, that you may not come into temptation' " (verse 38). And then He lovingly makes allowances for them, probably in response to stammered apologies. " 'The spirit is willing, but the flesh is weak' " (verse 38).

At the moment, that statement is true of Himself, too. So He takes His own advice and makes His way back to His place of prayer. The battle is not yet won. Dare I wonder aloud whether their weakness and selfishness has made it even more necessary that He pray for God to give Him strength to be willing to save them whether they deserve it or not? Surely the devil whispers something about how little they merit such suffering.

Satan also sees to it that they fall promptly back to sleep. And I must not deceive myself—I would have slept, too.

Again Jesus gasps out His prayers, pleading with God to take the cup away, to let the hour pass Him by. Again the devil makes it seem to Him, in His weakened condition, that perhaps He really could be mistaken about all this; maybe there really is some other way to save us all. But Jesus knows the difference between "seeming" and "reality." God, who always answers prayer, answers His Son's prayer with tears in His own voice, too. In His heart, Jesus hears it. "No, My Son, this is the only way." And again, Jesus comes with decision to the bottom line. " 'Not My will, but Thine be done' " (Luke 22:42).

Jesus goes again to His disciples and finds them sleeping, this time unable to apologize, feeling so guilty they don't know how to answer Him.

For the third time, He manages to stagger away before He falls to the ground. Again He prays the same prayer, and again His decision stands unbroken. The devil's fury knows no bounds. If this Emissary of heaven is going to be broken, He must be made weaker. The devil pours on the physical agony, causing Jesus' face to be twisted beyond recognition; great drops of blood fall like sweat. He pounds home Jesus' greatest fear—the one that makes nails, whips, and curses seem as nothing at all.

"You know what it means—complete separation from God, the utter, howling darkness of hell, with me! You'll never survive it. It is impossible! A third of the Trinity, once torn away, could never be replaced!"

There it is, the leering, monstrous specter of the only thing Jesus has ever really feared. What if it's true? It might be. But even if it is, He faces it and gasps out one last time, "Thy . . . will . . . be . . . done."

36

At this moment, it looks as though Jesus might actually die, but God gives a nod to one of the countless hovering angels, all weeping with their overmastering desire to *do* something. Like a flash of personified joy, that privileged one appears and gathers up his fallen Commander into strong, loving arms, wiping the blood from His face, whispering words of courage and comfort. Watch Jesus, trembling with pain and fatigue, cling with joy and relief to this dear friend. Listen! From the heart of the Father to the heart of His Son, on the lips of a ministering angel, there comes the message, "Well done, My Beloved!" Perhaps the angel reminds Jesus of one of His favorite promises: "You shall see the fruit of the anguish of Your soul, and be satisfied. It will all be worth it, my Lord!" (see Isaiah 53:11).

We can only begin to guess what it means to Jesus! The angel helps Him stand, and with one last embrace, and maybe the whispered assurance, "As thy days, so shall thy strength be" (Deuteronomy 33:25, KJV), he vanishes. But he doesn't go far. Though I can't see them, I feel sure that every angel who could be there that night was there.

For the third time, Jesus patiently wakes His disciples. " 'Are you still sleeping and taking your rest? It is enough; the hour has come; behold, the Son of Man is being betrayed into the hands of sinners. Arise, let us be going; behold, the one who betrays Me is at hand' " (Mark 14:41, 42).

He turns to face Judas, His familiar friend, one whom He has loved and still loves—and look at His face! As always, prayer has given Jesus the steadfastness and courage He needs to go on. His face is marked and lined with His suffering, but His eyes are at peace.

The battle has been won. The trial and the Cross have yet to be faced, but Jesus fought and won His fight of faith in the Garden. He

6

He Dies for Me

Of all the scenes on which anyone could meditate, the Crucifixion is the most painful and horrible. In itself, it is the most terrible thing the universe has ever beheld—or ever will. More than that, each human being who ever contemplates the Cross must also realize that had they been the only person who ever sinned, Jesus would have done it all, just for them. Even if they—chilling thought—still turned it down.

Think of it! Just for me. Just for you.

That is why the Crucifixion is even more important than it is terrible. Calvary is the pivot around which the universe, and most especially our world, turns. If we expect to begin to understand and relate to our small selves God's unspeakable, astonishing love for us, this is the place to start. In preparation, please read Matthew 27:31-54; Mark 15:20-39; Luke 23:26-47; and John 19:17-30.

Setting

A dim, steep street in Jerusalem, now known, with good reason, as the Via Dolorosa, or Sorrowful Way. Golgotha: a bleak hill not far outside the city.

Devotional Retreats

Background

Since Gethsemane, Jesus has spent the rest of the night and well into the morning in bodily torment; His friends have deserted Him; His enemies abuse Him. There has been a ridiculous farce of a trial, and He has been condemned to die at the hands of Roman torturers. Now He staggers up the street, longing for the moment when it will all be over.

*   *   *

Noise. I am surrounded, hemmed in, hammered on by noise and unwashed bodies. Voices shout curses, taunts, and ridicule. Hands reach for stones and throw them at the limping, bleeding, exhausted Savior. Too often, they hit their mark and cause fresh bruises and cuts.

And I am one of the cruel ones. Yes. It is the most horrible thing about this meditation, but it is true. *I* have shouted at Him, argued with Him, told Him to leave me alone, even taunted Him with being only a man, after all, and powerless to save Himself or me, or even to help me with the annoying details of my selfish, petty life.

I have deliberately done and said things I knew would hurt Him—and left undone and unsaid things He trusted me to do or say for Him. I caused some of those lines you see in His tired face, some of the stoop to His young shoulders, some of the premature gray at His temples.

But worst of all is the knowledge that I am part of the reason for those great, bloody welts on His back, the thorn-gashes on His brow. I am one of the ones who shout, "Crucify Him! Get rid of Him! I don't want to see my guilt mirrored in His blameless, loving face anymore!"

But, praise God, I still have choices. I don't have to be His enemy. I can choose to be His friend.

So I am also one of the weeping women, caught in a terrified grief greater than any we have known before. All our lives we have seen daring Jews put to death by these soldiers. Some of us have lost beloved family members and friends to the cruel sword of Rome. Perhaps there are even those among us whose babies died at Roman hands thirty-odd years ago. But *this* Man? He was going to change it all! Everything would be different. He was going to set up a new kingdom under God with liberty and justice for all. It is impossible that He, too, should die. I won't believe it. If it is true, all my hopes, my life, will end too.

I gaze despairingly toward heaven. The sun is bright; the birds cheerful. How can the earth simply go on? Where is Jehovah now?

But Jesus turns and looks at us—at me. " 'Daughters of Jerusalem, stop weeping for Me, but weep for yourselves and for your children. For behold, the days are coming when they will say, "Blessed are the barren, and the wombs that never bore, and the breasts that never nursed." Then they will begin TO SAY TO THE MOUNTAINS, "FALL ON US," AND TO THE HILLS, "COVER US." For if they do these things in the green tree, what will happen in the dry?' " (Luke 23:28-30).

I can barely see Him through my tears, barely hear Him over the noise of the crowd. What on earth does He mean? That worse things will come than this? Impossible!

The soldiers shove Him roughly, and He stumbles on. The next time He falls, the cross is transferred to a strong bystander, and all too soon we reach the desolate hill chosen for the execution.

Here is the worst moment we face. I can't watch. I hide my eyes, but I can't close my ears. I hear the hammer blows, the shrieks of the two criminals, the thud of the crosses going into their holes. But nothing from Jesus.

I steal a terrified look through wet lashes. He hangs silent on the center cross, His face white and drawn, His eyes closed tightly in agony,

His hands and feet pouring fresh blood. I can't stand it. I feel I must surely run screaming and get Him down from there. But I only turn my head away again and cry more bitterly.

As they finish securing His cross, Jesus speaks. I press closer and look up at Him again. "Father, forgive them. They don't know what they're doing" (see verse 34).

Astounded, I don't turn away this time, but stare in fascinated bewilderment. Did He really say that? Did He mean me, too? Can it be possible that I can be forgiven for my part in this scene of horror?

Around me the din goes on. The soldiers are rolling dice for Jesus' clothing and mocking Him, offering Him sour wine, which He refuses, and saying, " 'If You are the King of the Jews, save Yourself!' " (verse 37). Even my own Jewish leaders standing nearby are calling, " 'He saved others; let Him save Himself if this is the Christ of God, His Chosen One' " (verse 35).

Encouraged by their rulers, the demonic raging of the crowd reaches a new height. The two criminals even join in—" 'Are You not the Christ? Save Yourself and us!' " (verse 39).

Jesus does not answer. Perhaps He is still praying, though He says nothing more. After a while, one of the criminals falls silent. Between gasps for breath, he seems to be trying to see Jesus' face. Finally he shouts at the other thief to be silent. " 'Do you not even fear God, since you are under the same sentence of condemnation? . . . we are receiving what we deserve for our deeds; but this man has done nothing wrong.' " Turning again to Jesus, he says in a different, humble voice, " 'Jesus, remember me when You come in Your kingdom!' " (verses 40-42).

I stare. And then—can it be? There is a shadow of the old, familiar smile on the Master's bloodstained face. "I can promise you right now— you will be with Me in Paradise" (see verse 43). Just like that! The same assurance and authority as ever!

He Dies for Me

The crowd quiets a moment, uneasily. I and the women around me feel our hearts a little reassured, in spite of everything. Is He then still the One of our hopes? Can He still save others, though He chooses not to save Himself? The look on that thief's face is enough to brighten the whole landscape. With blood falling from his own hands and feet, ending a life of crime and hatred, *he* believes! Is he right?

Jesus turns His head painfully and looks down at us. I follow His gaze and see Mary, His mother, as close to her Boy as she can get, feeling every pain He feels. He smiles again, tenderly, and consigns her to the care of John, His only disciple who has dared to come so close. Spent, He closes His eyes, and Mary's shoulders sag a little lower under their load of pain.

It is noon now, and a sudden and terrifying darkness descends upon us. It's as if Jesus' Father, whose presence and concern I doubted an hour or two ago, can no longer stand to watch. Surely, of all the dark and evil deeds He has ever had to witness, this is the darkest. Perhaps He's going to destroy the earth and all of us with it. Even the crowd is silent, and some run away in terror. I tremble, but I cannot leave.

Three interminable hours pass. The darkness and the smell of death and blood are oppressive. At last it frightens even Jesus. He cries out, " 'MY GOD, MY GOD, WHY HAST THOU FORSAKEN ME?' " (Mark 15:34), and I can hear His mother's heartbroken sobs begin anew.

A few more jibes come out of the darkness.

"He's calling for Elijah."

"Let's see whether Elijah will save Him!" And some half-hearted laughter.

But neither fear, nor darkness, nor pain can dent Jesus' unwavering trust. " 'Father, INTO THY HANDS I COMMIT MY SPIRIT' " (Luke 23:46). With a loud cry, He is gone.

Gone! It is over, and the Light of my life is snuffed out. Then, adding to my shock, I hear the centurion begin to praise God and say, " 'Truly this was the Son of God!' " (Matthew 27:54).

I am stunned. In the hour of His death, at the end of all things, I have seen the salvation of Jesus work its wonders on two seemingly impossible cases—one a criminal, and one the very man under whose orders Jesus was hung on the cross. The one who gave the directions, maybe the very one whose hands wielded the hammer!

If He died for them, then He died for me. The stones and the taunts and the disobedience are forgiven! But what does it mean? Is it worth anything?

Jesus is dead.

7

He Lives for Me

If the death of Christ was the darkest day in the history of sin, then surely His resurrection was the brightest. Yet, though few friends were aware of His birth, few present for His baptism, and few at His death, *not one* was present at, or aware of, His resurrection! Not one! After all His clear predictions, the only people who remembered were the priests, and their response was to set a heavy guard and worry all night. Not a single follower of Jesus waited up and watched for His vindication—as far as we know.

And what a scene they missed! We are going to pretend to be some unknown person who really did see it happen, but neither your imagination nor mine will come close to doing justice to the actual, incredible event. In preparation, please read Matthew 28:1-11; Mark 16:1-11; Luke 24:1-12; and John 20:1-18.

Note: It's obvious that those who wrote these accounts were so head-over-heels with excitement at the time that it was impossible for them to remember all the details exactly. This can make the Resurrection a complicated subject on which to meditate. There are two possible solutions. One is to choose the account that speaks to you most powerfully and just concentrate on that one. The other is to find an account that harmonizes the Resurrection stories of all four Gospels into a coherent whole—such as the one I have chosen in *The Desire of Ages* by Ellen White.

Background

The death and burial of God's only Son was not entirely ignominious. During the hours He was dying as a criminal among criminals, two men had seen the salvation of God, and seeds had been planted in many other hearts. After His death, when His criminal status would have called for His burial in the common field reserved for such and the peasants who loved Him could do nothing, two other men came forward and saw to it that He received a bit of the honor that He deserved.

Joseph of Arimathea provided a new tomb and a burial cloth and got permission from Pilate to take the body. Nicodemus provided about a hundred pounds of burial spices. With their own hands, these two wealthy, influential followers of Jesus tenderly took His tortured body down from the cross, wrapped it with the spices, and laid it sadly away. The women helped and saw to it that everything that could be done for their beloved Lord was done, then went home to prepare more spices and ointments. The priests set their seal and their guard, locked their doors, and chewed their nails.

Sabbath came.

*   *   *

It is night. Sabbath is over. But then, as far as we are all concerned, it has been night since He . . . What a horrible Sabbath it has been! Sabbath was a joyless burden for so many of us for so long—until He came. Oh, what I would give to see that smile, those merry eyes! And now . . . back to business as usual.

The Passover sun has shone as brightly as ever all day. It's hard to believe. The sanctuary has continued on as it always has, though there has been a good deal of murmuring and speculation about that hastily mended veil. The hardest thing to bear has been the sound of the sick in the temple court who have come miles for Jesus' touch, and keep begging for Him.

And the children! They've cried for Him all day, and won't be put off. How can we tell them the truth?

That it is all over.

That we were wrong.

That He is gone from us forever.

No! How *can* that be the truth? It just can't be!

Last night, all I could do was cry. Today, I just want to make it through the day. But tomorrow we're going to get together and search the Scriptures. Perhaps God will have mercy on us and show us were we went wrong and what to do now. But, oh, how can we go on without Him?

I think I'd rather die.

* * *

Well, I seem to have made it almost through another eternal night. At least it surely has been long enough for three nights, though there are as yet no signs of dawn. King David said, "Weeping may tarry for the night, but joy comes with the morning" (Psalm 30:5, RSV). I wonder if he ever went through anything like this. My eyes ache. My head aches. Everything aches.

I can't stand it. I'm going over to the tomb.

As I enter the garden, which holds the sealed tomb, I pull my mantle around me against the cold and walk as silently as possible. I can hear the shuffling movements and weary sighs of the soldiers, and the last thing I want is for them to see me. I top a slight hill-ock, covered with trees and bushes, and find myself a place where

I can see that cold, silent stone, but not be seen myself.

As I stare, the tears begin again. Why am I here, anyway? Do I think I can somehow convince myself that it's really true that my Friend is in there, silent, unmoving, that His great heart has actually stopped beating and that He will never smile at me again?

Impossible. Yet I cannot go. So I stay, growing cold and stiff as the darkness continues. Will dawn ever come?

Suddenly, I'm shocked into full awareness as, with no warning of any kind, several things happen at once. There is a flash of light so brilliant that both hands fly up to cover my eyes. A violent earthquake throws me to the ground; all the guards shout terrified curses and then are silent. Heart pounding, I peer through shaking fingers.

The guards are scattered about the ground as though dead, and at the tomb a being so bright I can hardly make him out is rolling aside the great sealed stone as if it were a pebble. I stare in fascinated shock.

At the open door of the tomb, the being stands aside and calls in strong, clear tones that fairly quiver with joy, "Jesus, Thy Father calls Thee!"

There is a stir, and forth from the tomb comes—Someone! Is that Jesus? Gone is the lowly Galilean Carpenter! This Man is a King! With the assured step of a victor, the Lord steps forth from His temporarily borrowed resting place.

This scarcely seems to be the same person as the sorrowing, fragile human who pled with His Father for strength three nights past. His eyes meet those of the angel with a gleam of joyful reunion, and then that mighty one—perhaps the same one who held up his fainting Master in the Garden—falls to his knees in humble adoration before the King of heaven and earth.

I, in my hiding place, feel as though my heart has stopped and forgotten to start again. I cannot even comprehend it all yet. I can only stare as Jesus neatly folds the grave clothes and leaves. The angel assumes a less alarming form, and the soldiers come to their senses, stare at the empty tomb, and race away as fast as their terrified feet can carry them.

Moments later, as streaks of sunrise (at last!) begin to appear in the sky, another solitary figure enters the garden. It is Mary Magdalene, weeping as she comes, longing only to be near Him in death, as she has been near Him in life. But she sees the stone rolled away and the empty tomb and races away, sobbing, just missing meeting the rest of the women who have come to finish embalming Jesus' body.

As they walk, I can hear them wondering aloud, "Who will roll away the stone for us? It is far too large for us to move."

Then they, too, see that the stone has already been moved. They also notice a young man in white sitting on it. They are frightened, but the angel says, " 'Do not be afraid; for I know that you are looking for Jesus who has been crucified. He is not here, for He has risen, just as He said. Come, see the place where He was lying' " (Matthew 28:5, 6). Trembling with wonder, the women come closer, and the angel continues, " 'And go quickly and tell His disciples that He has risen from the dead; and behold, He is going before you into Galilee, there you will see Him; behold, I have told you' " (verse 7).

The women enter the tomb, and inside is another angel who asks, " 'Why do you seek the living One among the dead? He is not here, but He has risen. Remember how He spoke to you while He was still in Galilee, saying that the Son of Man must be delivered into the hands of sinful men and be crucified, and the third day rise again' " (Luke 24:5-7).

The women stare at each other, first in astonishment, then in rising excitement. That *is* what He said! They rush away, laughter and joyful praise mingling with the morning praise of the birds. The disciples must be told! He is risen!

The garden is destined to be a busy place this morning. Moments

after the women's excited voices have faded, Mary comes back, leading Peter and John. For some reason they do not see the angels. But
they see the empty tomb and the grave clothes and go away wondering.

Mary remains behind, crying. Isn't it bad enough to lose Him to
death, without losing His body, too?

The angels speak to her this time. " 'Woman, why are you
weeping?' "

" 'Because,' " Mary sobs, " 'they have taken away my Lord, and I
do not know where they have laid Him.' " Not to be consoled, she
turns away.

It is then that Jesus does something He doesn't do for anyone else.
His heart must long for heaven and His Father's arms, but He has
lingered just to speak to Mary.

She perceives someone dimly through her tears, hears the question
again. " 'Woman, why are you weeping? Whom are you seeking?' "

" 'Sir,' " wails Mary, " 'if you have carried Him away, tell me where
you have laid Him, and I will take Him away.' "

It's an amazing thing. The smile of Jesus the King and Conqueror
is the same gentle smile as that of the beloved Carpenter. " 'Mary!' "

Mary turns with a gasp. " 'Rabboni! [Teacher!]' " A world of meaning, a wealth of friendship and understanding is encompassed in that
word. Mary, with long practice of hanging on Jesus' every word, com-
prehends all in a flash and begins to throw her arms about Him.

But Jesus, stops her (though with a smile, I'm sure) and says,
" 'Stop clinging to Me, for I have not yet ascended to the Father; but
go to My brethren, and say to them, "I ascend to My Father and your
Father, and My God and your God." ' "

What a message of comfort! I can see Mary pausing for one long,
last look at Him before turning away and running to tell the disciples,
" 'I have seen the Lord' " (John 20:13-18)!

It is the greatest message they will hear that day. The others can say, "The angels said . . ." or "The tomb is empty!" Only Mary can say, "I have seen Him!"

You and I can say that, too. And if those who hear scoff and say, "How can you claim to have a relationship with Someone who lived 2,000 years ago?" well, we are not alone. The disciples, His own disciples, thought the women were hysterical. Especially Mary.

So be it. Their doubt does not harm the truth.

I have seen Him! He lives! And I am free forever. He has carried all my sin, paid the price in full, and now He will reign eternally—and I shall be right at His side.

8

He Gives Me Repentance

In the story of any one soul's salvation, it is easy to think that step one is repentance, step two, conversion, and then comes salvation. The reverse is actually the truth. Salvation comes first of all. Isaiah tells of God begging the unconverted person to " 'return to Me, for I *have* redeemed you' " (Isaiah 44:22, italics supplied).

This was nearly six hundred years before Jesus even died! But the moment sin entered the world and the Holy Godhead contracted to execute the plan of salvation, it was as good as done. That's why the Bible calls Jesus "the Lamb slain from the foundation of the world" (Revelation 13:8, KJV).

God always acts first. We must never lose sight of this great truth. He seeks and finds me and grants me spiritual healing so that I may see how truly desperate my situation is and cry out for help. Then He tells me the good news: " 'Do not fear, for I have redeemed you; I have called you by name; you are Mine!' " (Isaiah 43:1).

Only then can He give me the gift of repentance—the ability to see how tirelessly He loves me, how much He has done for me, and that heartache is all I have given Him in return—so that I will turn back to Him.

In all the Bible, my favorite example of this ongoing process is found in the story of my dear brother, Peter.

This is a drama in three acts. The first occurs just before Gethsemane (Matthew 26:31-35; Mark 14:27-31; and Luke 22:31-34). Act Two comes during the trial itself (Matthew 26:69-75; Mark 14:66-72; Luke 22:54-62; and John 18:15-18, 25-27). The finale is mentioned only in John 21:15-17.

Peter is someone who, as the saying goes, requires no introduction. Nearly everyone feels at least some affinity with him, even those who are not blessed/afflicted with an impetuous, opinionated, emotional personality like his.

It is very beneficial for this meditation, however, to spend just a few minutes going over the roller-coaster emotions Peter had already experienced on the night of Act One.

First, there was another episode of the ongoing "who-is-the-greatest" argument. I feel sure Peter's voice was one of the loudest, no matter what view he espoused. Then there was Jesus' demonstration of the humility He expected of them. In two seconds, Peter went from the height of pride to the depths of humility—and no doubt began feeling miserably guilty over his earlier arguing. Next, the emotion-laden scene in which Jesus first declared there was a betrayer in their midst, ("Lord, *surely* it couldn't be me?") and then unmasked him and sent him out, unrepentant, to fulfill his plans. Peter was probably shocked and angry and would have been delighted to "teach Judas a lesson." But then, like the others, perhaps he decided Jesus had just sent Judas out on an errand, after all, since Jesus calmly, though sadly, went on eating and talking to them of many things.

Now they're at one of their favorite places—the Mount of Olives—and poor Peter has had quite a wearing night already.

* * *

Act One:

I am tired and confused. And cold. Why are we still wandering around at this hour? Not that it hasn't been great. One of the closest times we've ever had together. He has told us such things! Since Judas left. But some of it made no sense. He kept talking about His body being broken and His blood being shed. And betrayal. I swear, if that holier-than-thou Judas. . . ! "What? Me? I mean, yes, Lord?"

" 'Satan has demanded *permission* to sift you like wheat; but I have prayed for you, that your faith may not fail; and you, when once you have turned again, strengthen your brothers' " (Luke 22:31, 32).

I swear, I cannot understand half of what He says tonight! It sounds like the story of Job or something—Satan demanding permission. And I *am* converted! Still, the idea of Jesus praying for me makes me feel somehow small and humble.

What was that? We'll all turn away from Him tonight? He'll see His prayers for *me* are not wasted! " 'Lord, with You I am ready to go both to prison and to death!' " (verse 33).

Now what is there to smile about in that? I mean it! Not that it will be necessary. He is God's Anointed, after all. The others all agree with me. Maybe we're all just a little loud about it, to cover up our uneasy feelings tonight, but we all mean it. He's got plenty of protectors with us around! Especially me!

"Even though all these others may fall away because of You, I will never fall away. Not even if I die!"

But Jesus only says, "I tell you, this very night, before the cock crows twice, you will deny that you even know Me three times" (see Mark 14:29-31).

It's impossible. It's absurd. Not that I would ever lay blame on the Master, but I must admit I'm a little hurt by His obvious lack of trust in me. I never thought He would say such things to one of His closest friends.

I can hardly concentrate on all these things He's telling us. About being the Vine, with us as branches, and about peace and joy and mansions! But what in the world is all this about going away, and not seeing Him, and then seeing Him again? And leaving the world and going to the Father. I think I'll ask Him to explain it all more clearly another time. This is such a weird night. We're all too tired to think clearly.

Even Jesus! He seems so . . . I can't explain it. Troubled by something, and sad. It's as if He's withdrawn from us in some way and yet reaching out to be closer to us than ever before; both at the same time, somehow. It sounds crazy. We're all just tired. And worried. Could it be possible that there's a plot on the Master's life and that He knows it? Not that it would be the first time.

Why doesn't Jesus *do* something? *Brrr.* I'm glad I have my cloak. And my sword. Just in case.

Act Two:

(In between, Peter has been unable to stay awake with Jesus. Feeling guilty about that, he tried to protect Him with the sword, was rebuked for it, ran away in a panic, and then, with John, followed at a distance as Jesus' captors took Him to the high priest's house.)

This is just unbelievable! I can't believe it's really happening. And Judas—that . . . !

I'm not afraid, but I keep wondering when Jesus is going to show His power and get out of this mess.

Jesus is right. All the others have fled for their lives. Cowards! Of course, John and I ran at first, too, just for a minute, in the panic of the situation. But we soon got hold of ourselves, and we won't be easily shaken now. We got into the courtyard. John knows the high priest. The slave girl who kept the door asked me if I was one of Jesus' disciples, but I played it cool and said No. Better to be a little discreet just now. I wouldn't want them to keep me away from Him right when He needs me.

It's really getting cold. In the center of the courtyard there's a brazier with a charcoal fire in it, where the soldiers and slaves are keeping a little warm. I think I'll go mingle. I wonder what hour it is? The night should be practically over. I just heard the first cock's crow of the morning.

They're getting rough with Jesus. How dare they? I could just kill them all. But what could one man do? They'd just beat me, too.

"No, I am *not* one of His disciples!"

"No, I don't even know the Man!" (see Mark 14:66-72).

Persistent, these nosy fools! I felt the anger growing, and before I realized it, out came a stream of that sailor-talk I thought I had finally vanquished once and for all.

There goes that rooster again. Oh, God, what have I done? With a guilty shock, I glance over at Jesus.

He is looking right at me. It's a look I shall never forget to my dying day. How could He turn and look so compassionately at me while being mistreated by stuffed-shirt priests and Roman boors? I wish I could die!

* * *

Peter rushes from the place weeping as he has never wept before in all his blundering, boisterous life. He cries the rest of the night away, feeling that, after all his boasting, his sin is too great to be forgiven. Or at least, he will never have his position of trust among Jesus' friends again. Have you ever sinned like that? Felt that way? Remember it, and feel Peter's pain.

He Gives Me Repentance

Act Three:

(The scene changes completely. It has been more than a week since the Resurrection, and Peter has been subdued and quiet all that time. With some of his friends, he has just been fishing all night without success. Then Jesus has appeared on the shore and helped them to net a great catch.

As soon as he realizes who it is, Peter, who can't stand being separated from Jesus anymore, dives in and swims to shore. Perhaps he has helped Jesus with the breakfast preparations. Now they have finished breakfast and are just enjoying the presence of the dear Friend they lost—and regained.)

*   *   *

I wish I could just sit here with Him forever. This is the third time He has appeared to all of us, as a group, and He has yet to say anything resembling "I told you so" concerning the night of His arrest. Even though He was right about all of us, except John.

Especially me. I hate myself.

But I love Him. I love Him!

After we have finished eating, He turns to me. "Simon Bar-Jonas." (Here it comes, but I can't quite fathom that slow, knowing smile.) "Do you love Me"—He gestures to the others—"more than these?"

Feeling thoroughly ashamed, I drop my eyes. "You know I love You, Lord."

His answer is strange: "Tend My lambs."

Then He asks again, "Simon Bar-Jonas, do you love Me?"

Well, I can see why He wouldn't believe me. "Yes, Lord, You know I love You."

"Shepherd My sheep."

I look up at Him, but He is gazing out to sea with an inscrutable look on His face. A third time He asks the same question:

"Simon Bar-Jonas, do you love Me?"

I was right; He'll never trust me again. "Lord," (I am ashamed of the babyish quiver in my voice) "You know all things; You know that I love You."

Again He answers, this time looking at me, "Tend My sheep."

I meet His eyes. He smiles that incredible smile of His, and my eyes fill suddenly with tears, for now I realize—I am forgiven! (see John 21:15-17).

All at once I understand. Three times, on that night of horrors, I was asked if I loved Him, and I said No. And it was true. I mean, yes, I did love Him, but . . . well, I loved myself better. Three times *He* has asked me if I love Him, and the answer now is "YES!"

Unbelievable as it seems, I think He actually considers my fall to have made me capable of taking on a new commission! Something I know I would never have been able to do before—to feed His lambs, nurture His new little children into the faith.

Well, I'm not sure how good I'll be at it, but any job He says I can do, I'll do! Never again, by His grace, will He have cause to look at me the way He did that night.

Once is enough for a lifetime.

9

He Converts Me

Now Peter was really converted, for repentance and conversion go hand in hand. True conversion cannot happen without repentance, and true repentance automatically brings a desire to change, to have a selfish way of life converted into a Christlike life.

Absolutely anyone may be converted by Jesus, if he or she chooses to be—a fact which causes continual surprise, if not disapproval, among unconverted Christians.

A perfect example of this is found in Luke 19:1-10.

Background

This is another story that occurs during the last few days of Jesus' life on earth. It happens in Jericho, a city rich in the history of God's mighty acts. Jesus has told His disciples that they are on their way to Jerusalem so that the prophecies concerning His arrest and death may be accomplished. They have not understood Him, of course.

Zaccheus is the chief tax collector of Jericho. Tax collectors are despised as a class—and with good reason. They collect taxes (which the Jews abhor the necessity of paying in the first place) for Rome

59

(which the Jews abhor as well), and on top of that, they add heavy surcharges for their own enrichment. One may well imagine the disgust with which the citizens look upon one who has clawed his way to the top in such a profession.

But Zaccheus is not all as he appears to be. He has heard of the teachings of John the Baptist, who baptized in the Jordan near Jericho. He has heard of Jesus before, too. Now he hears that Jesus is actually coming to his hometown.

*   *   *

I must see Him. I must. Nobody would understand, so I don't speak of it. But I *must* see Him.

I suppose it's probably nothing. Just another in a long line of "messiahs." But His message is so different from the rest. I've heard so much about Him. He seems to be one of those rare people who don't just speak endlessly of love, but who really do love—even people like me, or so I've heard.

Of course, He'll never even notice me. Nobody does. Until it comes time to pay up, that is. Then I *make* them notice me. Still . . . I wonder if He really means what He says about loving your enemies? Maybe He wouldn't say that if He knew as much about enemies as I do. Or maybe He would. I'll know, if only I can see His face. Just see Him.

The crowd is impossible. It's shoulder-to-shoulder; homespun and sweat next to Tyrian purple or Oriental silk and perfume. It's Passover Week, and the overflow from Jerusalem fills all the cities around her skirts. Beautiful Jericho is the resort of choice for those travelers who did not arrive in time to find lodging in the Mother City herself, but who can still afford to be choosy. And still they act like a bunch of children in the marketplace or a Coliseum mob, shoving each other and shouting excitedly.

Then there are the sick and the beggars—worthless lot! They're always after Him, I hear. They smell to high heaven. And the children. If one more slams into me, I'll kick him!

I'm not so bad at elbowing my way through crowds, myself, but today looks impossible. I can't begin to get near, and I'd have to be right in His face to see Him, anyway. I'm such a puny excuse for a man. I don't want Him to see me.

If I could just see His face!

I know what I'll do! He's heading up the main street of town; He'll pass right under that wide-branched sycamore on the corner. I duck down a side street, pushing against the flow of humanity for a few breathless minutes, and finally find myself in a quiet back street.

The sound of the crowd is muffled now. No one is about but those few who aren't even curious enough to take a look at the much-discussed Preacher. Panting, I dart down the street several blocks and then back to the main street. Here is my corner. And no one is around to see me clambering up the tree with about as much dignity as an alley cat.

I try to dispose myself in as hidden a spot as possible while still keeping a view of the street below. I feel ridiculously conspicuous, but after all, nobody will be looking up. They won't notice me any more than they usually do.

As I wait on the mob's slow progress, I think back on some of the things I've heard that this Man says and on the preaching, a few years ago, of the late John the Baptist. He baptized in the Jordan right near here. I went to hear him a few times. He was a bit heavy on "repent and change your life." Still, I never could quite get his words out of my mind. "The kingdom is at hand!" Jesus says that a lot too, I believe.

Everyone says Jesus plans to set up some sort of kingdom now and kick out the Romans. That would put me out of a job, of course. But there are days when freedom would be worth everything I own.

I can hear the crowd getting louder and see them coming closer. In a few minutes I'll have a good view. All I ask is to look at His face and see there whether He really means what He says. I guess I'm asking for miracles. It's really pretty foolish—a man of my age and position, crouching up here on a limb with twigs sticking in my back, waiting for a chance to try to read somebody's mind!

Here He comes. It certainly is easy to pick Him out of the milling throng! From up here, He is its obvious center, the point toward which all the others lead and lean and point. And He's so quiet. Like the eye of a hurricane.

All around Him I can recognize the men who are His disciples by the way they act possessive and protective and try to keep people from suffocating Him. They're not noticeably successful. Children tug at His sleeves and skirts, and Jesus smiles down at them and bends to hear and answer them and give and receive indiscriminate hugs. How can He? I know some of those dirty faces. Brats and ruffians, old enough to know better than to throw rocks at a tax collector trying to make an honest living.

There's Joktan's wife with that sick infant of hers. I don't want to be harsh, but really! Can't her husband make her face reality? The poor thing would be better off dead. They'll have more of them soon enough. But the woman struggles and then bursts through restraining arms to run right into Jesus' shoulder with a force that would have made Him stagger if the press of humanity wasn't holding Him up. She backs away apologetically, but says something and holds out the baby. He actually takes it! I stare in fascinated disbelief as He holds it, caresses it, and gives it back, no longer crying. Surely He hasn't . . . I feel my heart speeding up in a dizzying way.

The mother is hysterical with joy, but cannot get out words of thanks before Jesus is clutched at from another direction by old Hadad with his lame leg and a ruffianly boy who seems only to want to touch Jesus and see His face. (I never thought to feel a sense of kinship with a street urchin!) Both also receive loving touches and smiles from Jesus, and the lame leg is healed. *Healed!* Hadad waves his cane in the air triumphantly, and the roar of the crowd grows in volume. But I can't take my eyes off the face of that boy. He backs away, but follows on. His newly squared shoulders and the look in his eyes declare without the need for words that here is one street boy who won't be throwing any more rocks and rotten fruit.

I am satisfied. It's not just His loving face, but every move He makes that shows His genuineness. Even I am determined to change, if it's still possible for an old thief like me.

He's nearly under me now. When He has passed, I'll drop down unobtrusively and . . . Oh, no! I can't believe it! He's looking right up at me, just as if He knew I was here! Of course, everyone else is following the direction of His gaze. My face burning scarlet, I drop my eyes, feeling like the greatest fool who ever lived, and wait for the shrieks of laughter.

But Jesus' voice rings out suddenly, clear and authoritative, forestalling any ridicule. " 'Zaccheus,' " (He knows my name!) " 'hurry and come down, for today I must stay at your house' " (Luke 19:5).

My house! Unable to trust my ears, I raise my eyes and stare at His upturned face. The corners of His eyes are crinkled in amusement, and His mouth smiles merrily. But in His eyes there is compassion and, yes, love! For me—the most despised (and despicable) person in Jericho. It's as if He knows every idiotic, selfish thing I've ever done— and loves me anyway.

I am frozen for a second that lasts an eternity, and then the laughter does begin. Jesus Himself begins it, and those near Him take it up. It's a different laughter, though, than any I've ever heard. My face reddens again with confusion, but I grin, too, as I clamber hastily down, hardly caring that hundreds of eyes watch my ignominious descent.

As I land at His side, I am aware suddenly of how tall He is. It's strange, but beside Him I don't feel the sting of my own small stature. For once, I feel ten feet tall!

"This way, Master!" I can scarcely contain my excitement as I stumble over myself to lead Him to my home. But then it begins. Maybe those who would ridicule me had also been momentarily speechless. But now the murmurs and glares start to multiply.

Jesus ignores them, so I try to follow His lead. But by the time we reach my doorstep, the anger is obvious and easily audible. "He has gone in to be the guest of a man who is a sinner."

Instead of my usual burning sense of bitter injustice (Who do they think they are, anyway?), I feel humiliation and sorrow. It's true, after all. My neighbors know very well of whom they speak. I steal a shame-faced, sideways look at Jesus' face. Very likely, He does not realize who and what I am, or He would not have chosen to honor my house, beautified as it is by ill-gotten wealth.

But He is looking straight back at me. And without His saying a word aloud, I hear, "I know who you are, Zaccheus Tax-Collector. Nothing you could tell Me would surprise Me. Hold up your head, My son. I love you!" All in a look! Never have I met a Man like this.

I turn suddenly and face Him squarely, head up, but hands shaking. Jesus glances over the people, and they quiet abruptly. In an unfamiliar, humble voice, I make my declaration. " 'Behold, Lord, half of my possessions I will give to the poor, and if I have defrauded anyone of anything, I will give back four times as much' " (verse 8). I can hardly believe I am saying such things. I can see the crowd doesn't believe it at all.

But Jesus smiles that dazzling smile that could call the sun out of the sky and says, " 'Today salvation has come to this house, because he, too, is a son of Abraham. For the Son of Man has come to seek and to save that which was lost' " (verses 9, 10).

We manage to make it into the house and shut the door on the dumbfounded faces just before I burst into tears. And before my Lord leaves this house, I know I am indeed the richest man in Jericho.

10

He Builds My Faith

If there is one thing a newly converted child of God needs more than anything else, it is faith. Satan and his angels shriek with outrage almost as loudly as the courts of heaven ring with joy when one is saved from his evil clutches. We may be sure that he will do all in his power to convince the newborn believer to return to old, ingrained ways of thinking and lose faith.

But be of good cheer. Faith, also, is a gift of God (see Romans 12:3; 1 Corinthians 12:7; Ephesians 4:7). We shouldn't be surprised to learn this. Everything else has been a gift of God so far, and the Bible says *"Every* perfect gift is from above" (James 1:17, italics supplied). Yet somehow, we often believe that faith is our part—what we produce in response to Gods' grace—when, in fact, faith is what God produces in us as part of His grace, if we allow Him.

Allow Him. What does that mean? How do we accept the gift of faith? Once again, the Bible has the answer: "So then faith cometh by hearing, and hearing by the word of God." (Romans 10:17, KJV) It's really as simple as it sounds. The best way to hold on to the faith God has given—and to strengthen and increase it—is to study the Word of

God. If we look back and see what He has done, we'll see that He has never yet been wrong or let His children down.

King David shows us how to do it in Psalms 105 and 106. His advice to us there is: "Seek the LORD and his strength, seek his presence continually! Remember the wonderful works that he has done, his miracles, and the judgments he uttered, O offspring of Abraham his servant, sons of Jacob, his chosen ones!" (Psalm 105:4-6, RSV).

If you read and meditate on all of Psalms 105 and 106, you will find them to be the story, in miniature, of all God's dealings with His people—as well as a giant lesson to every child of His. Psalm 106 is the story of the troubles Israel brought on herself by lack of faith. "They quickly forgot His works; they did not wait for His counsel" (verse 13). Centuries of tragedy followed, with interludes of blessing whenever "they believed His words; [and] sang His praise" (verse 12).

Those old stories have just as much value for you and me—spiritual Israel (see Galatians 3:29)—as they did for the Israelites. Look in the Old Testament for meditation subjects, and you will find it filled to overflowing with vital pictures of God's glory, mercy, and love. Let your mind dwell on the Creation, the Flood, the stories of Joseph and the patriarchs, the captivity and the Exodus—then the wanderings! Try to imagine what it would really be like to walk under the guidance of a pillar of cloud and fire.

Ask God to show you, and you will discover there have been times when He *has* led you just as clearly as that and that He will do so more and more.

Study the feasts and the sanctuary. Ask your Teacher to show you what it all means to *you*. Watch the Israelites' bloody, erratic, incomplete conquest of the land God would have given them without all that trouble—if only they had been the light to the nations that He asked them to be.

Sit in on His centuries-long struggle to teach them to abhor idolatry and ask Him to cleanse all idolatry from your life. Weep with Jeremiah, hope with Isaiah, go into the Babylonian captivity with Daniel. Watch the miraculous conversion of the mighty Nebuchadnezzar and the downfall of Babylon (right on schedule)! Join the singing, weeping remnant of exiles on their way home—home!—to rebuild desolate Jerusalem, their Mother City. Study the prophecies of the coming Messiah, and those of the very last days.

Then imagine the difficulty I face in choosing just a few Old Testament meditations for these pages. I finally settled on four, which exemplify four of the titles of God: Creator, Deliverer, Vindicator, and Voice of instruction, guidance, and warning.

It is by beholding these mighty acts of our Almighty God that our faith becomes strong, well-grounded, and able to face and overcome even the strongest of temptations and delusions. If a God like that is for us, who indeed can be against us?

11

Faith in a Creator

The entire Bible, the entire plan of salvation, the entire history of a small planet somewhere on the fringes of the Milky Way Galaxy, are centered around only three events: the Creation, Jesus' life, death, and resurrection on earth, and the Second Coming. I believe a proper understanding of the first is vital to a real comprehension of the other two. It is impossible to see the Bible as the story it claims to be—even to see God as the Being He claims to be—without looking at the whole story in light of a personal, hands-on creation of the universe by a Father-God.

In preparation for this truly spectacular meditation, please read Genesis 1:1–2:3.

Background

Yes, even for this story there is a background because there is an important question, one that has been asked over and over: *Why* did God create this world, especially if He knew what would happen? This question is easily the subject for a full-length, in-depth Bible study and meditation all by itself. We will deal with it only very briefly here.

There is one simple answer to that question, and it is an answer that profoundly affects our view of God and of ourselves. It's found in several places in the Bible, but the major passage is Isaiah 43. (You may easily use cross-references and pursue the subject further, if you wish.) Notice verses 1, 2, 7, and 21 of Isaiah 43, especially verse 7 in which God says He created us for His glory.

What is God's glory? When Moses asked God that very question (see Exodus 33:18), God showed him His character. " 'The LORD, the LORD God, compassionate and gracious, slow to anger, and abounding in lovingkindness and truth' " (Exodus 34:6). The conclusion is obvious. If God formed us for His glory, and if His glory is His character of love, then He formed us for love.

God lives in a Trinity, a unity of complete love and oneness. But that wasn't enough for Him. The angels were created before our world, and apparently other worlds were, too. But even they weren't enough. He wanted still more children to love. He wanted you!

Not only did He want to love, He wanted to be loved, as well. Since we are formed in His image and our greatest need is to love and be loved, then it follows that God's greatest need is to love and be loved—by you and me. Incredible, isn't it?

With that in mind, let's watch God build a world.

Note: There is a lot of controversy in some circles over what happened on the fourth day of Creation. Why would He wait and make the sun and moon on that day when light was created on the first day? I can't imagine. Perhaps the heavenly lights were visible for the first time only on that day? Who knows? To avoid all controversy, I have imagined this creation story in exactly the order it was written. Rearranging details doesn't change the fact, or reduce the awe, that the hand of God did it all. He was the only One there, and if He says it took Him a week, I would think He ought to know!

Faith in a Creator

*   *   *

It is dark. We are surrounded by a darkness unlike any we have ever imagined before. It's almost a tangible, touchable thing, this heavy, black night. And so silent. Not a sound, not a breath, not a whisper anywhere.

Gradually, we become aware of a Presence. Without sound or sight, it's difficult to tell how we know, but we know. Someone is here—a joyfully thoughtful Being, planning, planning. We can sense the anticipation, the excitement.

A Voice speaks. " 'Let there be light' " (Genesis 1:3)! Only four little words, but the very sound and power of the Voice takes over, filling and transcending all the infinity of silent darkness, and—as if the very Voice itself is light or becomes light—there is light!

Only light. A strange, cold light. The dawning of a world.

With no sun " 'to separate the day from the night' " (verse 14), we must take God's word for it that there is an evening and a morning, the first day.

The second evening and morning come, and the Voice speaks again. " 'Let there be an expanse in the midst of the waters, and let it separate the waters from the waters' " (verse 6). Again, the words become what they speak, and the silent, formless waters suddenly have an atmosphere. Clouds above, water below, and air between. A breeze stirs the water for the first time, and we hear the lapping of the waves and discover what an astonishing amount of difference air alone can make. Sound, wind, vibration, the ever-changing clouds—all because of air!

The evening of the third day arrives, and then the morning, and we sense a new thrill of anticipation in the hovering Presence of God, as if today great things will happen.

" 'Let the waters below the heavens be gathered into one place, and let the dry land appear' " (verse 9). With a mighty, rushing roar, the great deep gathers itself aside to its ordained boundaries. New, wet earth raises its head and settles into mountains, valleys, and plains all beautiful in the grace of their flowing lines. With awe we watch the giant upheaval, seeing that it is all under control.

The Master Sculptor works with His medium skillfully—a little higher here, wider there, setting limits for the waters. When He is through, the young world is already breathtaking in her beauty, with no adornment save light and shadow, line and texture.

But God is not finished. Again His majestic voice commands, " 'Let the earth sprout vegetation, plants yielding seed, *and* fruit trees bearing fruit after their kind, with seed in them, on the earth' " (verse 11).

With a new delight, we watch what these words become. The hills and valleys carpet themselves with lush, green grass that invites romping and relaxing. Hills are mantled in dark, rich evergreens. Great shade trees wave joyful branches. Ferns nod over rivulets. Wild flowers tremble shyly at the feet of slender birches and graceful willows.

Fruit trees offer their armfuls of bounty. Herbs and vegetables spread luxuriously over the fields. Just for fun, God flings handfuls of merry daffodils and noble irises, hangs veils of climbing roses and jasmine.

What a sight! What smells! One day is long enough to get only a fragment of a glimpse at this bright new creation. All too soon it is over, and the fourth evening begins.

But this night we will see a display that is unmatched—our first vision of that part of God's creativity, which for thousands of years will call to the heart of the most rebellious human with the nagging possibility that there is a God, after all.

Tonight, God says, " 'Let there be lights in the expanse of the heavens to separate the day from the night, and let them be for signs, and for seasons, and for days and years; and let them be for lights in the expanse of the heavens to give light on the earth' " (verses 14, 15).

Chills race up and down our backs as we gaze with breathless astonishment and rapture upon the myriads of stars and suns and wheeling galaxies. Children as we are of a polluted planet, we are awed into speechlessness at the clarity and brilliance of a universe unfogged, unsmogged, unclouded by millennia of evil and decay.

I could stare all night—how about you? But we are distracted by a new thing nearby. God has set a great, silver globe in the sky to rule the night. What a moon! We have to remind ourselves to breathe.

Then dawn comes. God has saved the best for now. Rosy gleams reach across the sky, the water turns to molten gold, and before our eyes, a fiery, jubilant sun rises and flings his hosannas of warmth and light over all the new trees and bushes and flowers. Now we discover that the valleys and mountains and beaches and waves were not, after all, as beautiful as they could be. Now, they bring tears to our eyes. Think of it! The first sunrise!

The fourth day, and God's work is already done for the day. We have all the daylight hours just to contemplate it all and praise Him.

The fifth evening, a moonrise; the fifth morning, a dawn that surpasses the one before it. So far, every day has been better, and today is no exception. For today that Voice is both majestic and merry as it proclaims, " 'Let the waters teem with swarms of living creatures, and let birds fly above the earth in the open expanse of the heavens' " (verse 20).

How can I find words to describe such a scene? Instantly the waters are teeming with life, from tiny minnows, crabs, and shellfish to laughing dolphins and ponderous, intelligent whales. There are flashes of silver as here and there a fish leaps out of the water in sheer exuberance. We could spend forever just exploring the mystical, brilliant world within the clean, crystal clear, perfectly safe waters of the sea.

But this was only half of God's creative activity on this fifth day. The words "let birds fly" have loosed an explosion of movement and color and sound in the newborn world. Everywhere we look the birds have cheerfully taken over.

On the hillsides the cardinals are already busily searching for pine nuts. On the water, graceful swans glide softly past fat ducks; neon flamingoes and solemn herons stilt-walk about in the shallows. Noisy gulls dip and wheel, and dozens of trees are filled with the chattering, good-natured quarrels of sparrows and finches and jays. Warblers and canaries and thrushes practice their first songs of praise. Over them all, the eagles keep sharp-eyed watch as they ride the waves of the upper firmament.

Then God does something He has not done before. He blesses His creatures, saying, " 'Be fruitful and multiply, and fill the waters in the seas, and let birds multiply on the earth' " (verse 22). Contentment and satisfaction underlies every syllable.

The sixth evening comes, and then the third sunrise greets the sixth day.

" 'Let the earth bring forth living creatures after their kind: cattle and creeping things and beasts of the earth after their kind' " (verse 24). Today is like a repetition of yesterday—only in even more variety. As the Voice speaks, so it is, and now there are scampering, chattering squirrels and gentle, giant elephants, noble horses and shy rabbits, frisking dogs, wise-looking cats, and lively, silly monkeys. Our minds cannot begin to hold all we see. Each animal is perfect in itself and put into its perfect habitat.

There are slow turtles and slinky salamanders on stream banks, deer and bears and foxes in the woods, lions and zebras, giraffes and gazelles on the savannah. None of them hurt or destroy. Each has its place in God's perfect ecology and keeps to it with joy.

Now this once-formless rock is really a world, complete and perfect. But one thing is still missing. This green, young earth has a special purpose for being; like a lovely ring-setting of gold filigree, it awaits its jewels.

There is that Voice again. Yet it sounds different this time. The power, the joy, and the anticipation are still there, but there is a new note. It's a note of love and tenderness, a note of hope and eagerness, a note of . . . well, I'd have to call it vulnerability. That's what love means, and certainly God opened Himself up to untold pain and suffering when He went ahead, took the risk, and said eagerly, " 'Let Us make man in Our image, according to Our likeness; and let them rule over the fish of the sea and over the birds of the sky and over the cattle and over all the earth, and over every creeping thing that creeps on the earth' " (verse 26).

Then an unbelievable thing happens. God does not say, "Let there be a man; let there be a woman." No, He kneels beside a streambank, takes the clay He has created, and with His own gentle, loving hands, He forms a man. Our hearts stir at the sight of him—strong and noble looking, with the stamp of his Maker on his earthen face.

Into that body go the heart, lungs, stomach, and other organs; hundreds of bones, perfect muscles, miles of nerves and blood vessels, all designed to last forever without wearing out. Into that skull goes the most incredible of all God's creations—an odd looking object a few pounds in weight, which will run the human body and guide the destiny of its owner and of the human race itself.

For when our Father God gave us the freedom of choice, He put into the hands of the human race not only a little of Himself (awesome enough), but actually gave us power not only over ourselves, but over others, and even over Him. I am the only one who will decide whether God gets what He wants—to live in joy and love with me eternally—or whether He must mourn my loss forever.

When God has finished molding His first earthly son, He bends over and breathes into him some of His own breath of life. We catch our breath with wonder as the man becomes a living soul. He sits up, blinks, and looks into the face of his Maker—a privilege no human since has had in the fullness that Adam and Eve had it.

Look at the love and rejoicing in those two faces as they gaze at each other!

But Adam is not yet a complete image of God. God is a family name, our name for a Trinity who together form a unity. So also must the human race be if they are to reflect the image of God.

So God puts Adam into a deep sleep. He takes a rib and closes up its place with flesh. And out of that rib, He creates the perfect companion for Adam. She has a body like, and yet unlike, the man's. All the same muscles and organs and nerves. The same kind of brain, with the same powers for good or evil. And yet, how different and how surpassingly beautiful! Again God breathes His breath of life. Again there is the miracle of a living soul—His daughter!

Watch as Adam awakens. See the look of transcendent delight that passes between the two who are, like their God, equal and one. The best of love we have left on this marred planet is only a reflection of that love that first came from the hand of love Himself.

To this pair, too, God gives His blessing: " 'Be fruitful and multiply, and fill the earth, and subdue it; and rule over the fish of the sea and over the birds of the sky, and over every living thing that moves on the earth' " (verse 28). The first—and best—wedding!

Adam and Eve walk off arm-in-arm to explore their garden home and it is the end of the sixth day of Creation.

God looks over all His works, and He is very pleased. All is perfect, fresh from a Father's loving hand, and behold, it is very, very good.

As evening comes the seventh time, He gives His children (and Himself) one final gift. He blesses the seventh day and hallows it and rests from all His work. It will be a whole day in which to share the fruits of His labor with those for whom He has labored. Adam and Eve have nothing from which to rest, but God shares His rest with them, anyway. And certainly they have much to celebrate. More than we, with our clouded intellects, can imagine.

On this, the first Sabbath, the "morning stars [sing] together, and all the sons of God [shout] for joy" (Job 38:7), and there is no shadow of a cloud on the horizon to dim the rejoicing.

Except in the mind of the Father. He knows what will happen. But He has already decided it will be worth it if only He can share eternity with you.

12

Faith in a Deliverer

We, with our gifted hindsight, know what happened to God's perfect creation. We are not always so sure it has all been worth it. Sometimes we are positive it's not. That is why faith in a loving Creator must broaden and deepen into the next step—faith in a Deliverer.

If we believed only that God had created us and then gone out to lunch in the Andromeda galaxy, (there are people who believe that, more or less), then where is the basis for security or peace, much less joy? Then we could say to God with reason, "You blew it, God! Why did You create this festering mud hole, anyway? And why did *I* have to be born into it?"

Some people say, "God may be able to forgive us—the question is, can we forgive Him?" Is it blasphemy? Certainly it is. But if one does not know God the Deliverer, what else can one think?

Knowing the Deliverer changes the whole picture. God did not say, "I want more subjects, and if they choose to embrace what is wrong and plunge their whole world into darkness . . . well, that's a risk I'll have to take."

No. God is completely sovereign. He knew that not only could He keep evil in check, but that for those who would let Him, He could actually turn evil into a brighter good than they would have had without darkness. He also knew that after only a few thousand years He would win back all His dominions. Then, with those of His children who now knew more about good and evil than those who had never fallen, He would form a celestial government that would never be overthrown or even threatened again (see Daniel 7:13, 14, 27).

God had a plan—a plan that would deliver anyone who chose to be delivered. It's what the entire Old Testament is about. In fact, it's what the entire Bible is about.

One good example of this theme is found in Exodus 14, the source of our next meditation. As I read, it helps me to remember the best description I have ever heard of "hardening of the heart." There is a lump of clay and a lump of wax. The sun shines on both equally, yet the clay hardens like a rock, while the wax melts and becomes pliable.

God would have been just as eager to give Pharaoh a new heart as anyone else, but Pharaoh refused. That being the case, God knew that the miracles He did to soften the hearts of His people would only harden Pharaoh's heart still further—and He said so. It was not a threat—only a prediction.

Background

The children of Israel are not yet such a unified group as the name suggests. They are a motley crew of thousands of lifelong slaves, together with some Egyptians who have been converted to the powerful God of these exiles. They have progressed only a very short distance on their journey.

Setting

The Sinai Peninsula is a rugged, barren land. The only fruitful places are near the few rivers. In Egypt, the Israelites have been well accustomed to the practice of irrigation. That's one reason why the promise of a "fruitful land of milk and honey" attracts them. But they have a long journey through rocky hills and flatlands before they will arrive at their longed-for Canaan.

The Israelites cannot get lost in this wasteland, however, for they are guided by God Himself, through the visible manifestation of a pillar of cloud by day and of fire by night. Still they can find cause to complain, for they have camped exactly where God told them to, in front of "Pi-hahiroth, between Migdol and the sea, . . . in front of Baalzephon," and now they are right in the middle of what appears to be big trouble.

*   *   *

I knew I would regret coming on this ill-begotten expedition. Who is this old man Moses, anyway? Only an ex-slave who can do a few magic tricks. He left Egypt (a fugitive from justice, no less!) before I was even born. Now he comes back with some tale of a burning bush that doesn't burn and a message from a half-forgotten god of a long-dead ancestor and stirs us up so that we actually lose our senses and leave the only security we have—to run away into this desolate wilderness from Pharaoh. Of course he's coming after us! What heat sickness got into our brains to make us think he wouldn't?

I can see how the Israelites would get all excited over the idea of a deliverer, but *I* have no part with them. I'm here only because, well . . . that's my son over there, the one with the curly hair. He's all I've got, and when he and his friend, Benjamin, begged and pleaded that I put up that silly blood on the doorposts, I gave in. And there he is, and here we are. If only he doesn't get killed anyway.

We are all supposedly equipped for battle, but what do slaves, or peasants, like me know of battle against the mighty chariots of Pharaoh? Here we are, a horde of wailing, terrified children, stuck neatly between the sea, the high wilderness on each side, and an angry Pharaoh with an expert army. I suppose there must not have been enough graves in Egypt to hold us all!

Still, that Moses certainly has charisma. All around me is wailing, moaning, shrieking, and trembling. Yet, he wishes to say something, and somehow he is getting this whole mob to gradually look at him and settle down.

It's hard to believe, but I think if that baby over there will just quiet down, I may be able to hear him, myself. I think I'll try to get a little closer. I have to admit, I've never been so petrified in my life, and if he has any sort of a plan, I want to hear it.

" 'Do not fear! Stand by and see the salvation of the Lord which He will accomplish for you today; for the Egyptians whom you have seen today, you will never see them again forever.' " (Oh, no, not platitudes and magic tricks again!) " 'The Lord will fight for you while you keep silent' " (Exodus 14:13, 14). Well, you can't doubt that *he* certainly believes it. I wonder where he learned to talk with such calm certainty in the face of a crisis of these proportions? Maybe he is crazy.

Wait! Something is happening. The pillar of cloud that's been up ahead is moving to the rear of us. Now that's strange. It's getting dark, too. Maybe at least the army won't be able to find us until morning. Small comfort, but I'll take any delay!

Now what is Moses doing? He's stretching out his arm or something—oh, it's that famous rod of his! I knew it—another display of magic. I wonder what he thinks he's doing?

Well, I'm not going to worry about it. I'm going to try to find a bit of a hiding place among the rocks and get some rest, even if I can't sleep all night. They won't take me without a fight! Now where is that boy? The children don't even seem afraid. Wish I had their blind trust.

. . . I knew I wouldn't be able to sleep. Ram is snoring gently away at my side, but I am so nervous that every sound makes me jump. Anyway, the noise of all the other scared, sleepless people and that awful, dry, east wind buffeting ceaselessly off the desert is enough to banish sleep. What an uncomfortable, pointless journey this has turned out to be. Well, I suppose tomorrow will see the end of it. I would not mind so much if it were not for Ram!

It is almost morning. I must have slept a little, after all, from sheer exhaustion. Ram is no longer beside me, and as I start up from sleep, new terror possesses me. This is it. Even my bad dreams cannot compare with what I will see today. My heart pounds, my mouth is dry, and I can barely stand up to gaze back and try to see or hear the chariots. But the pillar of cloud is still there, and Pharaoh's men don't seem to have discovered us yet.

Here, thanks be to the gods, comes Ram. But what is this he is babbling? The sea has done *what?* The boy drags me along, and I follow unwillingly. The whole rabble must have lost their wits from fear. They're all insisting the same thing. As we crowd past, I hear bits of chattering: "Yes, really! Jethro saw it! A wall on one side and one on the other . . . "

Now I see Moses giving the signal to go forward! The army will follow us. What is the point of all this?

Sure enough, slowly, jerkily, the multitude begins to gather up its belongings and move forward. It's complete chaos. Nobody is sure what's going on. Mothers chase down stray children, and the animal herders and their barking dogs are hard put to control their charges who can sense the fear in the air and have been restless all night.

Our section begins to move forward. I confess to a burning curiosity about what really is ahead.

Faith in a Deliverer

The minutes drag by as the unwieldy throng moves forward, slowly at first, then more quickly. The sounds filtering back now are distinctly excited and amazed. I have to keep a tight hold on my son, or he would be off in a flash.

I don't believe my eyes! But it certainly does look as though the vanguard is moving between two tall walls of some sort!

At last we are there ourselves. Ram is silent for once. My emotions are an indescribable mixture of astonishment, relief, and doubt. Am I dreaming? But I can feel Ram's tight grip, and my sandals tread dry stony ground. To our right rises a towering, shimmering wall of green-blue water, and to our left another. I hang on to Ram and put one foot before the other in a blank daze. I know my mouth is hanging open as I stare to one side and then the other.

It is a sight we will never forget or fully be able to describe. No one but those who see it with us will ever believe it. The water moves and flows as if we were looking down on the surface of a lake, yet it does not come down upon us. The ground is not even muddy.

Ram is jumping up and down, but I am still in a daze by the time everyone has finally reached the other side. We all stand in awestruck silence and gaze back the way we have come—the adults, that is. The children are dancing, even as we see the Egyptian army thundering after us. But as they reach the middle of the sea, a strange thing begins to happen. The chariots are slowing, horses rearing, and soldiers shouting, as if the ground across which we walked so easily is suddenly very muddy. It looks as though the mighty forces of Egypt are actually panicking, trying to turn and retreat, and getting themselves all in disarray.

Out goes that rod again. Moses is stretching his hand over the sea, and with a crashing roar that makes me cover my ears, the walls of water come down as though they are glad to be relieved of the unusual effort of standing against gravity. Every last soldier of the army is gone, buried.

Ram and his friends are war-whooping.

Moses turns, and his wise old eyes survey the crowd with a look that makes me feel as ashamed as a naughty child.

" 'The Lord is my strength
and song,
and He has become my salvation;
this is my God,
and I will praise Him' "
(Exodus 15:2)

We are delivered without lifting a finger. I will never doubt Moses' God again.

Never.

13

Faith in a Vindicator

It is hard enough to deal with our own recurring doubts, let alone the scornful doubts of those around us. In fact, there is only one way I know to face down the jeers of the world, and that is to let my faith in a Creator and Deliverer develop into faith in a Vindicator. This is something that I have only recently come to understand in my own life, and I have found it to be an exciting concept.

The Old Testament deals extensively with the idea of God as a Judge and Vindicator in favor of His people. Many of the psalms, most notably Psalm 37, bewail the fact that the wicked seem so often to be in the ascendancy—then firmly declare that it will not always be so. That, in fact, it is not so now. "The Lord laughs at him [the wicked]" (verse 13). "The salvation of the righteous is from the LORD; He is their strength in time of trouble" (verse 39).

The major and minor prophets speak of the same truth. " 'No weapon that is formed against you shall prosper; . . . This is the heritage of the servants of the LORD, and their vindication is from Me,' declares the Lord" (Isaiah 54:17).

The fullest realization of these promises will take place on the day when our Redeemer comes again to rescue and vindicate us and destroy sin forever, although not before every knee bows before Him and confesses His eternal, unfailing justice (see Isaiah 45:23). But all Bible promises are also meant for the everyday vicissitudes of life on this planet.

Many things in life seem to continue in injustice forever. But if we will claim the promise and expect it to be fulfilled, there are also many times when God will vindicate us before the world and make our " 'light . . . rise in darkness' " (Isaiah 58:10) for the glory of His name. Those who work evil against us and laugh at our faith will see the truth and know that they are wrong.

The taking of Jericho, recorded in Joshua 6, was just such an occasion. It is also interesting to read, in Joshua 2, the circumstances leading up to this event and learn how God used a loving heathen woman and promised to deliver her. (If you like fascinating historical notes, compare Joshua 6:26 with 1 Kings 16:34.)

Background

At long, long last, the children of the children of Israel have grown to adulthood; they have actually reached the Promised Land. Moses, much beloved after forty years of fatherly leadership, has died and been succeeded by Joshua. God has sent His Spirit upon Joshua and built up his faith with some wonderful promises (see Joshua 1:5-9).

Through a miracle just like the one their parents experienced at the Red Sea, the people have crossed the Jordan River. Imagine their rejoicing and excitement! They have celebrated their first Passover in Canaan; the manna has ceased!

Now they camp near the first city God has promised to give into their hands. One would think they would be preparing for a siege. But then, God never does what one would think.

Setting

Don't think of a desert here. This land is not like Egypt, but is " 'a land of hills and valleys, [which] drinks water from the rain of heaven' " (Deuteronomy 11:11), and Jericho is in one of the best spots of all, a place of beautiful palm trees and lush vegetation near the Jordan. Remember those grapes the spies brought back, long ago in Joshua's youth (see Numbers 13:23)?

* * *

It has been almost a month now since the Israelite spies left my house, and the suspense is killing me. I'm really not sure why I hid them in the first place. We are all terrified of the Israelites. We have seen how their God works for them. The old story of the Red Sea was already well-known in these parts, though nobody was entirely sure it wasn't just that—an old story.

There are so many of them, and they are so fearless! I guess I thought it would be better to be on the winning side. My life so far has been a waste, anyway. What have I got to lose?

Since their visit, much has happened both around me and within me. For one thing, we now know the Red Sea story was no legend! Just a week after the spies had left my house, their God did the same thing again so that they could cross the Jordan!

Everyone in Jericho has completely lost heart and wits. The city is shut up as tightly as can be managed, and everyone goes about with fear in his heart. Even my family and I are frightened. Every day I check to see that the scarlet cord is still in my window. I hope they keep their word, these foreigners. They are bound to me by oath, but that will do me no good if I am dead!

It has also been noised around from town to town, by the intrepid few who dare to keep an eye on the invaders, that they celebrated some strange rituals and feasts while they were camped over at Gilgal. Even the king and his court are completely discomposed.

But it's the changes in myself that are the most disconcerting. In these days and weeks, I've had time to think about my life and this city in ways I haven't before. This is a very wicked city. Nobody should know that better than I, a street-walker, and yet I'm almost surprised to admit it. I don't know whether our family will be slaves or prisoners (if those two Israelites actually remember us), but I'm beginning to think that being a part of a people with a real God like that might be worth anything.

Their God! That's what has my head really spinning. It's as though He, or a Spirit sent from Him, has taken control of my thoughts lately. He is never far from my mind. I keep coming back to two things: the miracles He has done for them and the way those two spies talked, almost as if they thought their God knew and cared for them personally. Not that He'd ever take notice of a harlot, of course, but I wish I knew more.

But the most awful thing of all is what has been happening this week. For the past six days, every morning at dawn, the Israelites have been marching around the city. I know it sounds odd, but I have a good view of them from my window.

First is a large company of armed men, then seven men dressed in white, blowing ram's horn trumpets, then four more white-robed men carrying some large, covered object, and last, a huge company of people, all marching silently and with great solemnity. It's the eeriest thing. They march once all the way around the city, a little distance from the walls, making no sound except for the continual mournful wailing of the ram's horns, and then go back to camp. And that's the last we see or hear of them until the next morning.

At first the city was simply paralyzed with fear, expecting at any moment some supernatural manifestation—fire from heaven, or something—to destroy us all. But as the days have passed, and nothing has happened, it has become something of a joke. Fear expresses itself as coarse laughter and jeers, and then begins to dissipate, until many insist they were never frightened at all.

I still am. I have no intention of underestimating that God of theirs. But as those around me give way to mockery and relief, I've begun to wonder whether, after all, my imagination is just working overtime.

This seventh morning, everyone crowds to the windows and ramparts at the appointed time, and sure enough, there come our "friends," right on time. To the accompaniment of hisses and laughter from the walls, they make their silent way around the town, and we prepare to go about our business.

But wait! They are not turning around to go back to camp. They are going around again! I wonder why? The high amusement of the spectators is somewhat dampened, as the trumpets continue nonstop and the whole multitude continues to march calmly around us. A third circuit follows the second, and then a fourth.

The morning wears on, and eventually the crowd of watchers thins out as many, bored with trying to figure it all out, turn with a shrug to the business of the day. My family and I, not daring to go outside the door of my house, remain. Out of curiosity, I count the circuits. They are on their seventh round, and I can sense a new feeling in the ranks. They must be tired, but they seem to have taken on new life now. As they finish their seventh circuit, they stop, and the trumpets give a sudden long blast. Then the people raise a shout, that can probably be heard from Gilgal, for all the world as if they have gained a victory! It is—*Oh, God of heaven, save us!*

Before my frozen gaze, the walls of Jericho are simply crumbling to the ground! In abject panic, my family and I throw ourselves to the floor, covering our heads and shrieking. All I can hear is the mighty roar of crashing stone and tile—and my own screams. Our whole house is shaking violently.

Then there is sudden stillness. I raise my head and manage to crawl, shaking, back to the window with the scarlet cord. I can scarcely believe my eyes.

As far as I can see, all is rubble and destruction, and the hordes of Israel are pouring toward the fallen walls. Their God has vindicated them again. I cannot be very surprised.

No, the thing that passes comprehension is that of the entire wall around the city, the section that holds my house, the home of Rahab the ex-harlot, is the only bit left standing!

After all, it was not the word of the spies I had to depend on—it was the word of their God. Of *my* God. I didn't really trust. I was frightened and disbelieving by turns. I thought I must be insane . . . but I stayed in the house.

I, too, am vindicated. I shall serve this God for the rest of my days.

14

Faith in a God Who Speaks

The phrase "formed . . . for My glory" means being created for God to love. But it means something else, as well. It means, even more obviously, that we were intended to give God glory, to glorify Him. It seems strange, if not impossible, to think of weak human creatures somehow increasing God's already-infinite glory unless we remember that God's glory and His love are the same. To give God my love is to really give Him something He doesn't have, and couldn't have, without me!

Once God has created a people, delivered them from the mess into which they immediately plunge themselves, and, in spite of their continuing unworthiness, vindicated them before those who ridicule them, then there is a way in which that people can vindicate Him in return. They can do it by following Him.

There is a perennial conviction on this planet that following God is impossible. (We all know who said that first. And look where it got him!) It's certainly true that every individual in the world is a sinner and incapable of righteousness. It's also true that God's strength is made perfect in weakness (see 2 Corinthians 12:9).

Even more remarkable, God can take a whole group of weak, imperfect human beings, give them new hearts that love Him and love each other, and make of them a unity whose strengths and weaknesses complement each other so that it really does show His glory throughout the whole earth. He begged and begged Israel to let Him use her this way (see Psalm 22:27; Isaiah 46:6; 49:6; and many other texts.) He is asking the same thing of His people today.

How does all this tie in with faith in a God who speaks? Well, there's only one way to follow Someone you can't see—and that's by hearing Him. In the very beginning, God promised His covenant people that He would not leave them in darkness without a guide (see Deuteronomy 18:15-22). He promised to raise up prophets to be His mouthpieces, so that no one would have any excuse for not knowing His will for the people.

In Acts 3:22-26, Peter reminded his hearers of that promise and of the fact that all those prophets whom God had raised up had pointed forward to the ultimate Prophet—the revelation of God—Jesus Christ.

Every one of those prophets, up to and including Jesus and any messengers God has sent since, have had only one purpose in life—to show the truth about God's eternal love and thus draw God's people to glorify Him by returning to Him the love, honor, and obedience that is His due.

Every human could have listened. Some did. We all could listen today. And some do. Aside from anything God may choose to say specifically to today's people, He still speaks through the Old Testament prophets as well. He cries; He pleads; He loves; He promises immeasurable blessings. He utters warnings, stern rebukes, and when all else fails, He allows doom and desolation to teach their awful lessons.

A classic example is Jeremiah, the weeping prophet. Through Jeremiah, God pronounced some of His most terrible judgments; during Jeremiah's time He finally had to resort to the seventy-year

Babylonian captivity to turn the Israelites from idolatry. Yet through the same man, the sorrowing Father also cries, "But if you will not listen . . . My soul will sob in secret for *such* pride; and My eyes will bitterly weep and flow down with tears, because the flock of the LORD has been taken captive" (Jeremiah 13:17).

Our God is a God who speaks.

What would it be like to be one of His mouthpieces? If you would like to know, study Jeremiah's whole life—from reluctant youth with a tendency to blame God and doubt His dealings to mature prophet who speaks the word of God in love and boldness. We'll deal here only with his call. Please read Jeremiah 1:1-10; 17-19.

Background

Jeremiah lived in the priest-city of Anathoth. When he was called, he was about twenty years old, and King Josiah, who had ascended to the throne at the age of eight, was only twenty-one. Josiah had already done a great deal trying to lead his people to reform (see 2 Kings 22; 23). But the people of Judah, though at first they seemed to reform, simply would not really commit their lives to God. They had plenty of false prophets saying, "Don't worry, you are God's chosen people; nothing can happen to you." The people preferred to listen to them.

Jeremiah tells us nothing about where he was or what he was doing when the word of the Lord came to him. We are free to imagine the setting in any way we please.

* * *

Yahweh! Speaking to me!

My heart beats like a war drum, and my palms feel wet. I remember the story of Isaiah, who saw a vision of the courts of heaven and thought he would die because he had seen God. But what is this He is saying?

" 'Before I formed you in the womb I knew you, and before you were born I consecrated you' " (Jeremiah 1:5).

Me? I have a wild, momentary notion that He has gotten me mixed up with someone else. Consecrated me for what?

" 'I have appointed you a prophet to the nations' " (verse 5).

Oh, no! I can't be a prophet! What do I know about being a prophet? And what does He mean, "to the nations"? No other prophet has been told to prophesy to any other people than his own. I force words from my mouth, and they jerk out, dry-sounding.

"Ah, no, Lord God! I don't know how to speak; I'm only a youth!"

But He stops me. "Don't say, 'I am only a youth'; for you will go to all to whom I send you, and you shall speak whatever I command you to say" (see verses 6, 7).

I bow my head. It is His will. He *does* mean I shall prophesy to other nations—but with His words. (They will hate me.)

He knows my thoughts. " 'Do not be afraid of them, for I am with you to deliver you' " (verse 8).

I look up again and feel my fear receding. Then He reaches forth His holy hand to touch my very unholy mouth—a wonderful and awful experience! " 'Behold, I have put My words in your mouth. See, I have appointed you this day over the nations and over the kingdoms, to pluck up and to break down, to destroy and to overthrow, to build and to plant' " (verses 9, 10).

I am growing frightened again. Not very reassuring words, these. They really will hate me. But after He has shown me strange visions of an almond rod and a boiling pot and declared troubling judgments against Judah, He ends with promises.

" 'Now, gird up your loins, and arise, and speak to them all which I command you. Do not be dismayed before them, lest I dismay you before them. Now behold, I have made you today as a fortified city, and as a pillar of iron and as walls of bronze against the whole land, to the kings of Judah, to its princes, to its priests and to the people of the land. And they will fight against you, but they will not overcome you, for I am with you to deliver you' " (verses 17-19).

And He is gone. All seems dark, bereft of His brightness.

I can't help wishing He had chosen someone else. But I am His to command. I don't want to let Him down. May my words be His, and not mine, all the days of my life.

I wonder, will prophesying make me tremble as I am trembling now?

No matter. He promised to protect me. Whom shall I fear?

Yahweh has spoken.

15

He Forgives Me . . . Again

In the past five chapters, we have dealt mostly with God's relationships with a people, a nation, a race. But all that is true of His dealings with His children as a whole is also true of His dealings with individuals.

As a person is "found," and saved, and forgiven by God, and as that person looks back on God's work in her past, faith grows. God's new child begins to believe that He really means what He says, that He really can give her complete victory, keep her from falling, and present her without a blemish for His glory (see Jude 24).

Unfortunately, what happens next is almost inevitable—not that it *has* to happen, not that God hasn't enough grace and power to keep it from happening, but it almost always does happen, anyway.

Satan, who was furious at the first hint of conversion, is simply beside himself at the new evidences of growth. He redoubles his efforts to nip this thing in the bud. If he can get a person to disbelieve God's promises, he'll love it. But her faith is now too strong for a frontal attack, he'll try something else. Discouragement is a favorite of his.

If all else fails, he'll try to see to it that she is so involved with good works that she either neglects her own prayer life or begins to become proud of herself. When he has her all set up, he'll hit her right between the eyes with a liberal shot of her own, personal, favorite temptation. And down she goes, with a resounding crash. Or a whimper. He's not picky.

Now for the discouragement and depression. If he can, he'll get her to neglect her health, which makes his job much easier. One good "comforting" dose of sugar will go a long way.

Shrieks of demonic laughter assail her ears. "Look at the wonderful Christian now! What a joke! Whom do you think you're kidding?" Head hanging, she has to agree. She *is* a failure, a disgrace to God. To fall *again,* to *that* temptation of all temptations! Wasn't her conversion real? She waits for God to punish her as she deserves. And the next bad thing that happens to her she sees as the heavy hand of her Father.

Is this what is meant by the command to humble ourselves before God?

No. In doing that we deny our Christianity, and thereby deny Christ and His power. Jesus intends for us to realize the depth of our sin and to feel sorrow and remorse for turning from Him and causing Him pain. But He also intends for us to fly immediately to Him in confession and receive pardon, cleansing, and restoration.

" 'The spirit,' " He observed patiently, " 'is willing, but the flesh is weak' " (Matthew 26:41). But never apply that verse without also applying this one: " 'My strength is made perfect in weakness' " (2 Corinthians 12:9, NKJV).

He is able.

So what does one do when lying at the bottom of a pit of one's own making, especially when (as usually seems to be the case) it is a trap one has fallen into and been delivered from on at least seventy times seven other occasions? Is God's forgiveness used up?

Our next meditation is found in Luke 7:36-50.

Setting

There are two things to bear in mind. One is the Middle Eastern custom of washing the feet of one's guests. The other is the fact that in wealthy houses such as this, guests "reclined at the table," lying on couches raised at one end, with their feet out behind them.

*　*　*

I can feel my knees trembling as I creep into the room where my Lord is. I wait for a moment in a quiet corner, trying to get a better grip on myself.

Simon has outdone himself tonight. The long table is laden with food of every kind—rich pastries and imported delicacies next to platters heaped with grapes, figs, pomegranates, and perfectly-seasoned roasts. The table and wall sconces blaze with candles and lamps filled with the best aromatic oil, but the gleaming dishes and implements on the table, and the rich, colorful robes of the company seem to draw all the light so that the rest of the room is dim and shadowy by comparison.

Even in all this dazzle and display, Jesus stands out. My eyes are drawn naturally to Him, where He reclines on the resplendent couch in His simple Galilean robe. No heavy embroidery adorns His attire, no jewels flash on His fingers, no perfumed oils gleam from His hair and beard. He does not laugh and argue loudly as the other men do, yet He is the center of attention, as usual. How can I ever get near enough to give Him my gift without being seen?

It was all a foolish idea. I shouldn't have come. How can I be forgiven for such continued, unreformed sins as mine?

I have determined to do better so many times, especially since I've known Jesus and He has made me see that God could really forgive me. But here I am again, feeling discouraged and not at peace at all.

But I love Him so much. And I never would have, not in a million years, if He hadn't loved me first. He's done so much for me. I just have to do something in return. Something to show Him that I love Him, that His patience with me hasn't been in vain.

This perfume is probably a silly idea, but it was all I could think of. Others give such great gifts. I guess I'm just not that imaginative.

There. Some of the others are talking about something, and for a moment attention has shifted from Jesus. Maybe I can get to His feet at least. That stuffed shirt Simon didn't even have Jesus' feet washed, I noticed. Well, no one could help but notice! Here is Jesus, supposed to be the Honored Guest, but they're certainly careful not to touch Him. At heart, they all still consider themselves far above a mere Carpenter from Nazareth. Well, *He's* far above *my* touch.

Bowing over these dear, tired feet that walk miles of dusty roads every day so that sinners like me can know God's love and forgiveness, I feel tears begin to fall and pull my hair forward to hide my face. Worse yet, I didn't think to bring a cloth to wipe off the excess ointment, so my hair will have to do for that, too.

Oh, I knew this perfume was a bad idea! Its aroma has filled the room!

Maybe no one will notice over the smell of food and other perfumes. But I feel a stillness grow in the room and know I am discovered. If I could, I would escape, but I seem rooted to the spot, hiding behind my curtain of hair in agonized humiliation. I know what they're thinking, and they're right! How can He let a woman like me touch Him? Oh, that was the last thing I wanted to do—to bring shame to Him!

Jesus suddenly speaks, and at the sound of His voice, the whispers stop. "Simon, I have something to say to you." I can almost sense the

Pharisee look up with a guilty start. I push my hair back a bit and wipe away the tears so that I can see a little.

"What is it, Teacher?" Simon speaks in a voice of respect that is not quite respectful, somehow, especially when placed together with the lack of honor he has so far shown Jesus.

When the Master speaks again, it is in His storytelling manner, and He has the attention of everyone in the room.

"A certain moneylender had two debtors; one owed five hundred denarii, and the other fifty. When they were unable to repay, he graciously forgave them both. Which of them therefore will love him more?"

With apparent casualness, Jesus selects a grape from His plate, and the room is so silent I can hear a candle sputter.

By the look on his face, Simon is wondering if he has missed something. It seems a child's story. "I suppose the one whom he forgave more."

Jesus looks up and rivets Simon with His eyes. "You have judged correctly."

He turns to me, and I drop my eyes in a panic. But He speaks still to Simon. "Do you see this woman?" I tremble, and another tear makes a hot path down my cheek. "I entered your house; you gave Me no water for My feet, but she has wet My feet with her tears and wiped them with her hair. You gave Me no kiss, but she, since the time I came in, has not ceased to kiss my feet." (My cheeks burn.) "You did not anoint My head with oil, but she anointed My feet with perfume. For this reason I say to you, her sins, which are many, have been forgiven, for she loved much; but he who is forgiven little, loves little."

He looks at me again, and this time catches my eyes and holds them. "Your sins are forgiven."

I can't help it. I start to cry again. I hear the murmurs around the table start again. "Who is this, who even forgives sins?"

He Forgives Me ... Again

But my Master puts His hand on my head and says gently, "Your faith has saved you; go in peace" (see Luke 7:40-50).

I go.

And I am at peace.

Somehow, little by little, step by step, I will learn to hold on to His peace and His power and let Him really change my life.

I will!

*　　*　　*

It is possible. It must be possible. God says it is. If He says He can give us the victory, if He says He can change our lives, if He says He can deliver us not just from the guilt of our sin but from its power, then He can. But it is possible only in the warm and glowing climate of free, full, loving forgiveness. Forgiveness that continues longer than our sins continue. Forgiveness that we choose one time more than we choose to turn away.

God's forgiveness hasn't run out. He'll forgive you.

Again.

16

He Talks With Me

Once a converted, saved, growing, forgiven child of God learns how to see the Bible in a personal light and read all the precious old stories as if they really were written for him, then he is ready to discover the next step—how he can talk to God and hear God answer, just like all those people in the Scriptures did.

For Christians, this personal guidance from the Holy Spirit is second in value only to salvation, and Satan knows it. He is in the business of preventing souls from remaining in constant touch with their Father as Jesus was. It really is possible to be so connected. It was one of Jesus' last requests: " 'That they may *be one, just as We are one'* " (John 17:22, italics supplied).

How? There is only one way to the Father, and that is to stow away in Jesus, so that where He goes, you go. One extremely vital part of this abiding life is personal meditation. It's a way in which you, or any Christian, can go to God for guidance on personal problems or questions that the Bible doesn't deal with specifically or just to share the joys and trials of daily life and really hear an answer— just for you, just in your own heart.

But this becomes a rather unnerving matter. Isn't it possible merely to make up a conversation with God, inventing lines for Him that will feed your own will?

Yes, it is. The child of God who truly wants guidance will carefully guard himself from such possibilities by making full use of the armor God freely provides. He must become, through patient, prayerful study, firmly grounded in what God has already said in His Word. This means both practicing scriptural meditations such as the examples in this book and careful, systematic study of the themes and teachings of the Bible. God is never going to give you guidance that disagrees with His already-recorded Word.

You also must not forsake the fellowship of other growing Christians, especially those more experienced in their life with Christ. If you are perplexed or in doubt about something, check it with someone you trust and know to have a vital, experienced relationship with God.

But most of all, trust your Lord. Jesus is more concerned with keeping you from deception than you could ever be and is quite capable of protecting you if you just ask. So always, before any meditation, pray a prayer something like this: "Dear Father, I believe that You love me and want more than anything to guide and bless my life. I know that You have something to say to me today, and I want to hear You and nothing else. Please fill me with the Holy Spirit, as You have promised to do. Forgive my sins, take away my own wishes and desires, my doubts and worries, and protect me also from the devil's plans to harm me. I claim Your promise of wisdom, found in James 1:5, and the personal guidance You promise in Isaiah 30:21 and John 14:26 and 16:13. Help me to hear only Your message for me and to follow You throughout this day. Thank You for Your love. In Jesus' name, amen."

But in spite of all your prayer and preparation, and even though God is beside you and speaking to you, your meditations will still sometimes seem like mere imaginings—a child's daydreams. Don't be discouraged. That in itself is one of the devil's plans to harm you. Tell God your fears, too, and never give up.

Above all, remember this: "And the kingdom of God is like unto a radio network with a perfect transmitter and a great many very faulty receivers." No matter how perfect the transmitter (and it is), if I am not also a perfect receiver (and I am not, nor will I be until this world is ended and we are all put back on the same wavelength with God), there will sometimes be misunderstandings.

Never forget that, but don't let it throw you, either. God will not let you continue in a mistaken understanding as long as you stay tuned in. Keep checking back. Keep yourself conscious of His presence with you every moment of the day. With a humble realization of the frailty of your reception, keep your mind and heart open to Him, and "your ears will hear a word behind you, 'This is the way, walk in it,' whenever you turn to the right or to the left" (Isaiah 30:21). The High King of the universe has said it; never dare to doubt it. And the moment you are sure of His will, obey immediately. Hesitation will give the devil a chance to come up with all kinds of logical reasons why you shouldn't do it, and you will end up uncertain all over again about what your Teacher's will really is.

In this context, let me again recommend Morris Venden's book, *How To Know God's Will In Your Life*. Shall I tell you something funny? Well, not exactly funny. I wrote this chapter *before* the long journey I shared with you in the first chapter of this book. I knew all of this and believed it. Yet I still let my fears get the better of me. However, I always believed God before myself and assumed I was the one who was wrong. I did not, thank God, make the terrifying mistake of basing my life on what *I* thought God said, no matter how certain I was. Well, I wasn't certain! And my very uncertainty and unrest over the matter was God's voice, overruling my subjective understanding of what He had said to me.

I have known other people who, knowing this, have still gone to the other extreme and let one subjective experience define their spiritual lives—this despite the counsel of others and to their own eventual calamity. A man I'll call Bob was having an affair with the wife of another man whom we'll call John. When John, having talked to no avail with his wife, confronted Bob, Bob assured John that he had prayed very much over this matter and that God had assured him it was His will for Bob to leave his own wife and take John's instead! The Bible says, " 'The heart is more deceitful than all else and is desperately sick' " (Jeremiah 17:9). We all know it will go to any extreme to get its own way. I'm happy to report that Bob has returned to the Lord and understands his sin now. *He failed to put the Bible first above his own ideas.*

Some who have taken this route have never accepted correction. "God told me," they insist. Let me repeat: *God will not set aside His revealed Word, least of all His own law, to suit you!* We *must* keep a balance. And the principles outlined in Elder Venden's book can help.

A very good way to start personal meditation is by using nonaction Scripture as a springboard. God has declared through His servant Timothy that "all Scripture is inspired by God and profitable for teaching, for reproof, for correction, for training in righteousness; that the man of God may be adequate, equipped for every good work" (2 Timothy 3:16, 17). That's pretty comprehensive.

If you want to sharpen your mind, wrestle with Paul over a point of doctrine. If you want to increase your faith, meditate on the great scenes of the Old Testament. If you want to prepare for the future (and stretch your mental powers), study the tremendous prophecies of Daniel and John the Revelator.

If you want to learn how to meditate and how to deal with the tempest of feelings that tosses you about, go and sit at the feet of King David, a " 'man after [God's] own heart' " (1 Samuel 13:14) who was, believe me, just like you and me! I've heard people wonder why the Psalms are in the Bible. They are there because David, who wrote most of them, was the resident meditation expert of the Scriptures. He told God what he really felt in all kinds of situations, even when what he felt was outright wrong. And God has kept that record alive for us, in part to show us that we can tell Him anything at all and that He can help us to deal with it in a way that becomes positive and healing. You don't have to know much about the Psalms; just page through them until you find one to match your mood. Read it and study how David meditated, how he expressed his woes or his joys, and how God answered him. Notice that his complaints all begin and/ or end in praise. Always.

Then follow David's example. Talk to God yourself and hear Him comforting you or sharing your happiness. If you're angry, tell God about it, just as David did, and let God take your anger and show you how to constructively deal with whatever the real problem is.

There are many other passages, which are wonderful springboards to personal meditation. I love Isaiah, especially anything after Isaiah 40. Did you think those prophets spoke only for Israel? Try substituting your name wherever it says "Jerusalem," "Judah," or "Zion" and see if that changes your mind.

Our God stands ready to speak to us and guide us. If you'd like to hear Jesus Himself speak on the subject, read John 14 to 16. All we have to do is take His hand, trust Him, and quiet our spirits to hear His still, small voice.

He is knocking . . . and waiting.

He Walks With Me

As you move forward in the knowledge and love of God, you will grow and gain confidence; you will begin to know His voice and to feel troubled and wrong when you are moving against Him—and settled and right when you are doing His will.

Persevere, persevere; practice His presence: Sometimes He has no specific message for you, but just wants you to be still and calm at His side like two bosom friends who have no need of words, but only the bright warmth of their love for each other.

Then, sometimes you will know, with the depths of your heart, that the Holy Spirit Himself is in the room with you, and He will hand you a gem of wisdom on a silver platter—something you had never quite realized before or not in just that light. And you will understand suddenly that He loves you just as much as He loves Peter or Abraham or Mary or any of the favored ones with whom He spoke face to face.

Not long after I first began to practice this kind of meditation, I was going through a particularly troubled time in my life: It seemed as though sin had a hold over me that just couldn't be broken. I knew I was forgiven, but I was tired of being forgiven! I wanted to change! I felt as though I fought and fought and yet took ten steps backward for every three forward.

I now realize that this tormented time was to be expected; Satan hates meditation. You may expect just the same sort of difficulties. But then, that's why Jesus ended His pre-Gethsemane dissertation the way He did: " 'These things I have spoken to you, that in Me you may have peace. In the world you have tribulation, but take courage; I have overcome the world' " (John 16:33).

At the time, of course, I wasn't nearly so rational about it. In fact, as I recall, I was a pouting child of God, ready to throw a tantrum, when He came to me in the following meditation. It meant so much to me that I wrote it down as soon as it was over.

Please understand, this was not what is generally thought of as a vision or visitation. One of the ways I visualize the Christian life, in my mind, is as a climb up a narrow, rocky path, and Jesus simply took the pictures I habitually use and showed me His power in my life in a way I could understand.

He will use unique ways for each of His children. I offer this because it spoke to me in such a powerful way. I hope it may touch your heart as well and help you to understand what I am learning—that there would be an unfillable space in His heart without any one of us.

*   *   *

We are climbing.

We have been climbing for hours, years, lifetimes. The sun scorches my back and beats at the top of my head; hair and sweat are in my eyes, and my glasses perch maddeningly at the tip of my nose.

Before me is yet another harsh, loose-stoned rib of the mountain, steeper than any we have yet encountered, and my feet and hands blister at the mere thought of scrabbling up and still up. Only a tenacious sapling offers any chance of a hold, and I am reluctant to risk breaking its own hard-earned grasp on the rocky soil.

He is beside me, beyond me, knowing my distress without asking. I can hear His labored breath as He pulls Himself to a larger, stone-anchored tree above me. (Why is it that I always expect everything to be effortless for Him?)

"Just stay still a moment."

I need no second invitation; I gasp for breath and wait. He plants His feet firmly, grasps the tree, and leans down. "Here, take My hand."

I inch forward and collapse again, inches short. "I can't reach it!"

I push hair out of my eyes and feel like crying. I long for a drink or even a cool breeze.

His voice comes firmly, "It's a mountain we're climbing, you know. Did you think it would be like a stroll in the backyard? Just wait until you reach the top. It will be worth it, I promise you. Now stretch—I'm right here."

I sigh and raise my eyes from the cracked, dry soil to His face. He smiles, and everything is possible. I stretch.

"You must give Me the other hand, too. Let go of the rock."

I tremble, but watching His face, I let go and reach for Him. That strong hand! Calmly it pulls me up to fall beside Him under the tree.

Tenderly, He wipes my face, and I see blood on His hand where the tree has scraped it.

"Why do You do it, just for me?" I ask, touching the wound gently.

He smiles again. "Silly child! You're the only one of you I have!"

"And a good thing, too," I retort, half seriously, but He doesn't laugh.

His voice is almost sharp, and the smile is gone. "Never, never belittle yourself. You are Mine. I Myself have made you, and what I make is good!"

Tired, I dare to argue. I pick up a dead, worm-whittled leaf, so dry it crumbles a little in my hand.

"You made this, too, and once it was a beautiful leaf unlike any other. It is not beautiful now, and to say so is not to disparage Your work, but to recognize the work of another—a destroyer. This leaf is nothing now." I start to throw it aside, but His hand stops me with a stern movement and takes the leaf. Handling it with tenderness, so it will not break, He holds it to His lips for a second, then holds it out again.

My eyes are dazzled; my breath is gone. It is a glorious leaf, a prince among leaves! It is young, fresh, green with a green that catches the sun and shines luminously. I have never seen such a leaf!

After an age-long moment, I look up. His face is still stern, but His eyes are the eyes I have known from my cradle. They hold mine as He makes a gesture that includes all the world and says quietly, "In My hands lies the destiny of every leaf, twig, and stone in this valley. And doubt it not, My hands are strong enough to shape your destiny, too. There is absolutely nothing that the destroyer can do to make you or this leaf less than I choose you to be, as long as you are in My hands."

He holds them out. In one strong, gentle, scarred palm lies that leaf, shining, fairly vibrating with life. In the other, injured with helping me, I bury my face and weep. He lets me cry, then wipes away my tears.

I look down at the miniaturized landscape we have traversed and up at the terrifying, bigger-than-life vistas that are yet to be crossed, then back at His serene face.

"You said it will be worth it."

He nods.

I stretch my aching body and smile. "It's worth it now."

110

18

He Carries Me

" 'Then there will be a great tribulation, such as has not occurred since the beginning of the world until now, nor ever shall' " (Matthew 24:21). " 'False Christs and false prophets will arise and . . . mislead, if possible, even the elect' " (verse 24). "Therefore, take up the full armor of God, that you may be able to resist in the evil day, and having everything, to stand firm" (Ephesians 6:13). "The testing of your faith produces endurance" (James 1:3).

When I was young, I used to believe that by trials (which are all mere practice runs for the great tribulation that will come to God's children before He comes again) the Lord was training up a people whose faith would grow stronger and stronger until they could stand alone, no longer needing His hand to hold them up. I have since learned that this is exactly the opposite of the truth. Hear what God has to say about it: "Come, my people, enter into your rooms, and close your doors behind you; hide for a little while, until indignation runs *its* course" (Isaiah 26:20). " ' "Because you have kept the word of My perseverance, I also will keep you from the hour of testing, that *hour* which is about to come upon the whole world, to test those who dwell upon the earth. I am coming quickly;

hold fast what you have" ' " (Revelation 3:10, 11).

Where would a child of God hide? Where is He inviting us to hide? Not in any physical place. If God were not with His people right in the midst of the tribulation, why would Jesus warn us of the time or say that even the elect could be deceived or speak of patient endurance?

" 'O Jerusalem, Jerusalem, . . . How often I wanted to gather your children together, the way a hen gathers her chicks under her wings, and you were unwilling' " (Matthew 23:37).

How clearly I can see the tears of desolate sorrow in Jesus' eyes as He said that. May it not be said of me! "In the shadow of Thy wings I will take refuge, until destruction passes by" (Psalm 57:1). "For I know whom I have believed, and am persuaded that he is able to keep that which I have committed unto him against that day" (2 Timothy 1:12, KJV).

The Father is training a people whose faith will grow stronger and stronger until they are able to trust Him enough to let Him bear their weight completely on His wings. Then they will have unshakable peace in the midst of the storm.

Every trial that comes to a child of God can be used as practice until hiding in Him becomes second nature and even the great tribulation—though we can't begin to imagine how it will be when the devil truly brings all his ever-growing forces to bear on us—will have only the power to make us cling more tightly.

I was once plunged into a time of sorrow and despair such as I had never before imagined possible. It seemed as though nobody else in the world could hurt as terribly as I did, although I knew that what had happened to me happens to thousands every day in this sorrowing, old world. But the lessons I learned through meditation during this time of darkness are so precious that the words that follow are a very poor facsimile of the experience. I can only pray that my sharing them will enhance your own relationship with Him and lead you to lean ever more heavily on Him through your times of darkness.

*   *   *

We are no longer on the mountainside together. We must cross a ravine to reach another mountain, whose shape I cannot see through the mists and darkness. It looks like a horrible place.

"Oh, no, Lord, must we go there?" I cry.

"Don't be afraid, child. I have been there before. We will be together."

Through tears of desperation and panic, I gaze at what appears to be the only way to get there. Below us, the side of the ravine is filled with huge, sharp boulders, pits of quicksand, and thorn bushes. At the bottom rages a mighty, crashing torrent, the spray of its tortuous passing reaching up to where we stand.

The sun is hidden behind clouds blacker than night, and a violent storm is growing. The wind moans about us, rocking me where I stand. I hear thin voices and hints of faraway, mirthless laughter. Something moves, and I see snakes and wild, weird creatures disappear behind boulders and bushes.

"Is that the only way?"

He nods calmly. "It's the only way from here."

"Can't we go around, or . . . or something?"

"No, child."

In desolation of spirit, I throw myself into His arms and burst into wild tears. "I can't! I can't! I can never manage that path! I'll fall to my death! Can't we stay here?"

"For a little while. Come, sleep on My shoulder."

It takes a while.

He rocks me gently and whispers His precious promises and words of comfort. I feel the strength of His mighty arms around me and hear

His great, calm heart beating steadily against my ear. At last His gentle voice drowns out the doubts and fears that scurry through my head, and I sleep.

When I awake, it is darker still. Thunder crashes, and in the glare of frequent lightning I can glimpse the rushing torrent. Strange half-shapes hover just on the edge of sight and disappear when I try to look at them.

Fear grips me again, and I whisper, "I cannot, Master. Even if I have grown stronger through all the mountain climbing with You, You know I can't do this."

"I know you can't. I'm going to carry you. You will have nothing to do but to trust Me and hold still in My arms. You must not struggle or try to see where we're going.

"The way is difficult, but there is no need for you to be afraid. I have been here many times and can carry you easily if you are still and quiet. But if you struggle and cry out, you will make it slow going. The quieter you are, the stronger your faith will grow and the more quickly we'll get there."

He puts His fingers under my chin and turns my tearful gaze from the darkness to His face. In His eyes I see concern for me and sorrow for my pain, but not a jot of fear or worry. His brow is as serene as if we were off to pick flowers in a mountain meadow. My fear begins to ebb.

"Beloved, I know exactly how you feel. I cried the same frightened tears. I, too, begged My Father to let Me go around, or over, or any way but through the depths of the storm. I didn't think I could face the blackness of hell—of being without Him. Without Him!"

He closes His eyes for a moment at the memory, but opens them as calmly as ever. "Abba sent Me the faith and strength I needed, and I made it." He smiles. "Now you need never face that storm. In every storm you face, you are never alone. Look around!"

He Carries Me

I look. There are angels close around us, their wings rustling as they spread them about us to hold off some of the wind and the rain that is beginning. Their faces, too, are serene and strong. They never speak a word, and yet I seem to know that they are all saying cheerfully, "Don't you worry. This is nothing to Him. A snap of His fingers!"

I glance back again at the way we must go. "How would You like to snap Your fingers and make it all go away?" I suggest hopefully.

He smiles. "Then we'd miss the joy that is coming to us through this. You are more important to Me than a thousand storms."

He holds out His arms, and how can I be afraid? I give myself up to Him thankfully. Carrying me easily, He begins to make His steady way down the rocky path.

Path is the wrong word. It's nothing but a tumble of huge rocks and giant briars, but He never misses a step. Our progress seems slow to me, but it is sure and confident.

As we near the bottom, the storm worsens. Hailstones lash at us both, stinging our hands and faces, and we're drenched with rain and the spray from the river. The wind howls. It would surely knock me off my feet, and seems determined to wrest me even from His arms, but neither His step nor His grip on me is so much as shaken.

Worse than all this and the increasing roar of the water are the things I see and hear—the half-seen shapes of leering demons and the sound of shrieks of laughter and threats. Sometimes I hide my face in my Protector's shoulder, and He gives them a look that sends them howling for cover. Other times fear overcomes me, and I struggle and cry, which stops all progress until He comforts and calms me.

At last we begin to ford the river. I wonder whether perhaps it will part to let Him pass, but no. It seems that He intends to go right through every detail of this with me. As the foaming, frothing waves surge higher, I look around me again, and the tears of fright return. At the sight, the demons come close again, laughing and insulting.

I shiver and hear a whisper in my ear. "Sing!"

Startled, I look up and see my own special angel. "Look what He's going through for you! Look back and see how far He's brought you already. Sing Him a song of praise. It will lighten His heart and send the devils fleeing like the cowards they are."

I look at the One who carries me. His feet move forward confidently, but His eyes are on me. It's true; He deserves my praise. Why am I crying? Waveringly, through my tears, I raise my voice in the words of David: "My heart is steadfast, O God, my heart is steadfast; I will sing . . ." (Psalm 57:7).

My voice gains strength, and the results are overwhelming. My best Friend's face glows with a smile that banishes darkness. Demons flee shrieking, and fear leaves my heart as if I were a stranger to it.

Wonder of wonders, as we ford the deepest, loudest part of the flood, I hear my Redeemer's voice singing back to me! " 'Do not fear, for I have redeemed you; I have called you by name; you are Mine! When you pass through the waters, I will be with you; and through the rivers, they will not overflow you' " (Isaiah 43:1, 2). Right here in this cold, dark, angry place, my heart swells with inexpressible joy.

The river is wide. Time passes. Sometimes I still look around me and become frightened again. Sometimes I listen to the demonic suggestions and end up kicking and crying out again. Always He stops and quiets me.

I learn to be still and to sing. In return, He opens His treasures to me and strings blessings and promises like pearls and sapphires around my neck, flowing down to rest upon my heart.

As we reach the shore at last and He sets me down to begin the long climb up the next peak, I put my arms around His neck and begin to cry again.

He holds me gently. "What is it, little one?"

"Only that You were so right!" I sob. "Thank You for not snapping Your fingers and making it go away!"

His arms tighten around me, and our joy reaches heaven and flashes back from the Father to surround us with warmth and light. Around us I can hear the angels singing, and the storm and terror seem far away.

Now all we have is another mountain to climb, and what is that? We've done it before!

*   *   *

I tell you the truth. He has turned my mourning into dancing and fashioned me a crown of shining joy out of what I thought was a crown of thorns. Nothing, until I see Him face to face and feel His flesh-and-blood arms around me, will compare with the precious treasures He has given me in the midst of the darkest times of my life.

My brother, my sister, Jesus knows the taste of your sorrow. Hide yourself in His arms and let Him take you right through. You'll never regret it.

He Comes for Me

For those who learn to practice the continuous presence of God in their lives, trials become easier to take, even though they may get bigger and more terrible. These Christians come closer and closer to God until they live and move and have their being within the circle of His arms; nothing has the power to make them even consider moving from that place of safety, warmth, and perfect freedom.

The book of Revelation teaches that before Jesus comes again this "remnant" of people will "keep the commandments of God, and the faith of Jesus" (Revelation 14:12, KJV), that is, they will perfectly reflect the character of the Lord. How did they get that way? They accepted Jesus' life and death for themselves and His gift of eternal life. They then proceeded to "follow the Lamb wherever He goes" (Revelation 14:4). What a picture! They know where their happiness is found, and nothing can separate them from their Beloved. I want to belong to that group.

It is to these faithful ones that the promise is made, " ' "He who overcomes, I will grant to him to sit down with Me on My throne, as I also overcame and sat down with My Father on His throne" ' " (Revelation 3:21; see also Daniel 7, especially verses 14 and 27).

Best of all, these are the ones who will be alive to see the event for which the universe has waited so long. They will be the ones who hear that melodious Voice shout triumphantly, " 'It is done. I am the Alpha and the Omega, the beginning and the end. I will give to the one who thirsts from the spring of the water of life without cost. He who overcomes shall inherit these things, and I will be his God and he will be My son' " (Revelation 21:6, 7).

The Second Coming is the most exciting subject for meditation you could possibly have. Whenever I meditate on it, I always remember the verse, " 'He shall wipe away every tear' " (Revelation 21:4) and think with a smile that it means only tears of sorrow, fear, and pain. I think the Advent will be an event filled to overflowing with tears, which Jesus Himself will share—tears of overwhelming joy!

For pictures of the Second Coming from which to draw for your own meditation, see 1 Thessalonians 4:16, 17; Matthew 24:26, 30, 31; Mark 13:26, 27; Luke 17:24; John 14:1-3, 18; 16:20-22; Acts 1:9 (and I am sure there are many more!).

Background

The Second Coming is to be seen, in its fullest sense, not only as deliverance from this world and its horrors as we know it already, but as deliverance from the world as it will be during the time of the Great Tribulation. The persecution and evil, the great deception in 2 Thessalonians 2, and at last the physical falling apart of the earth itself (see Revelation 11:19; 16:17-21) are all terrifying to contemplate. Jesus said that if those days were not shortened, even the saved would not make it and no human being would be saved, but that for His children's sake, they would be brief (see Matthew 24:22; Mark 13:20).

Those who see Jesus come will see Him at the moment of their last extremity. They will have been through many times in their lives when they thought they would die if trials continued—only to discover it was not true. This time it will be true. But they will still know whom they have believed, and just before they lose their grip, their Deliverer will appear.

*   *   *

I never praised Him enough in the trials. I learned to cling to Him, to trust and praise Him—but not enough. Oh, my God, if ever I thanked You for the practice You gave me in singing in the dark, I thank You now! If ever I regretted the times I refused to drain the cup of woe and find its fullest blessing, it is now. Because those are the times Satan is bringing to my mind now. It is the practice I have in *not* thanking and trusting that he is making the most of. I am terrified and trembling, not sure of myself at all. But I am sure of You.

All around us is horror and death. Plague after plague has fallen. The antichrist has led the world to look to him and is now leading his followers to curse the remnant people who, he says, refuse to obey God (meaning himself) and so are the cause of the destruction and judgment falling upon the world.

God's children have been imprisoned; many have been killed, all in the name of God. Those who can do so have fled to the mountains and are hiding where they may. They endure privation and distress, but their bread and water are sure. They are the fortunate ones.

But all, no matter where, are being tormented by Satan. No one can hide from him—physically, that is. I can certainly hide my face in my Lord's shoulder, as I have learned to do! I can't feel His presence as clearly as I often have. But He has never failed me, and I know He is faithful and true. I know it. Over and over, through my tears, I sing again the promises that have carried me through before.

"You shall not be overwhelmed."

"Be of good cheer; I have overcome the world."

And most of all, "I am coming quickly!"

He Comes for Me

Oh, please hurry!

Everything seems so black . . . so cold. I can't hold on much longer.

At first, the storm seems only an outward manifestation of the inner torment of my soul. The wind tries to blow the trees over. The lightning tears the sky apart, and the thunder sounds like explosions. The earth trembles.

Then all hell breaks loose. The world is falling apart. Buildings crumble to the ground, and fires break out. Screams fill the air and something that sounds like . . . a trumpet?

I stare around me, uncomprehending, and suddenly I see an angel flashing toward me with outstretched arms. I recognize him as if I had seen his face every day of my life. My heart pounds.

"Is He really here?" I ask, as the angel sweeps me up into his arms. I surely must be dreaming again.

But my angel's voice is real and trembling with joy. "He is here!"

That's when I begin to cry.

As I am carried through the air, I can see around me that the sky is filled with angels, all carrying their own special little brothers and sisters to meet their Lord. The faithful dead of all the ages have been resurrected from their sleep and are up ahead of us, while "we who are alive and remain" (1 Thessalonians 4:17) bring up the rear.

On the tortured old earth, worn out at last by the weight of sin, the wicked shriek for the mountains to fall on them. For them, His coming is the last and greatest of all possible plagues.

But I have no eyes for the earth because up ahead, hovering in the clouds, waiting . . . there He is! There He really, truly is, at long, long last! His arms are outstretched as if to embrace the whole multitude of us all at once.

Soon every last one of His flock is gathered to His side, and we begin to ascend. The old earth and its horrors are left far behind in a moment.

Now the reunion begins. I can't begin to take in all that is happening around me. On every side, beautiful, re-created people weep in the arms of those they had lost; angels rejoice over those they sometimes despaired of ever keeping. There are the ex-widows and widowers in the arms of their lovers. I see David and Jonathan, laughing and crying by turns. There are Job and his children and the mothers of Bethlehem and Goshen, clasping their darlings as though they'll never let them go. There is my own bright-eyed baby niece, Alina, wet with the speechless tears of her mother and father. And here's my brother— so changed I hardly recognize him! His hug stops my breath.

But these are not the most blessed reunions. Those are taking place at the center of us all—the place toward which all eyes keep turning, the place where the tears and laughter begin.

See Adam and Eve in Jesus' arms, knowing that they were the ones who started us all on this long, sad, detour, but that their sin—all of our sin put together—was not as big as God's love and mercy, and that here we are reconciled.

Imagine His reunion with Abraham, Isaac, and Jacob, all looking young and vigorous. See Him exult over David and Job and Ruth and Naomi. See Esther stand before Him as once she stood before a much lesser monarch.

More exciting still, watch the reunion of Jesus and those who knew Him as a lowly carpenter. Look at the eleven staring at Him in awe. See Him laugh and grab big, dear Peter and beloved John, who is thinking that his visions didn't hold a candle to the real thing.

Oh, and look, there is His mother! As she cries in His arms, you can almost see her mind struggling with the paradox that this, her Lord and Maker, was once her Baby for a little while! The mystery of the Incarnation is one that will always capture the wonder of the universe. I think Mary will find it the strangest of all.

There is another Mary, too. If you ever want to find Mary

Magdalene when you're in heaven, just look for Jesus. There she will be. She won't hear Jesus say, "Don't cling to Me, Mary," this time.

But, for me, even these are not the most precious reunions. It is my turn. I haven't yet stopped crying tears of relief and transcendent joy (and fear that I am going to wake up any minute!). His face swims before me, and I'm sure my knees will not hold me up. But He reaches for me, and this time, this time, I can really feel His arms! They are stronger than I imagined, His face is more beautiful, and His scarred hands more gentle as He dries my eyes and murmurs, "What are these tears, My lamb? Did I not tell you we would make it?"

But I look up, and I smile because He is crying, too. The tears run down to His beard as He holds me to His heart and whispers, "At last, oh, at last!"

For you, too, there is yet another reunion—the best of all. It's your turn, now. Don't stint. Make it as wonderful and glorious and joyful as you possibly can. Stretch your mind to its highest height. You won't even come close. "Let your imagination picture the home of the saved, and remember that it will be more glorious than your brightest imagination can portray" (E. G. White, *The Faith I Live By*, p. 364).

Together, we all join hands and sing the song only those redeemed from earth can sing. The angels can only listen and celebrate.

He is really here!

It is really over!

Now, we can begin.

"And his servants shall worship him; they shall see his face, and his name shall be on their foreheads" (Revelation 22:3, 4, RSV).

"So we shall always be with the Lord" (1 Thessalonians 4:17, RSV).

"Amen. Even so, come, Lord Jesus" (Revelation 22:20, KJV)!

20

We Vindicate Him

In Nahum 1:9, we are assured that "affliction shall not rise up the second time" (KJV). In many other places, God promises to make a full end of sin (such as in Isaiah 24:20 and Jeremiah 51:64, which can be taken to apply to spiritual Babylon, the system of sin, as well as to literal Babylon). On the other hand, it is a complete mystery to all the universe why it ever occurred to Lucifer to sin in the first place. And I have sometimes wondered whether someone might someday get that notion to sin again.

Of course, it wouldn't be the same. If God had destroyed Lucifer as soon as it became obvious that he was determined never to repent, there would always have been some doubt—some obedience from fear rather than love. It had to be shown beyond the shadow of a doubt that God spoke the truth when He said sin leads to death. Now it has been shown. If sin arose in another heart, that person's sin could be allowed to destroy him or her immediately without anyone thinking that God was arbitrary or unjust.

But here's another way to think of it—just food for thought.

We Vindicate Him

One million years have passed since God created New Earth more beautiful than the first, and placed His universal headquarters, New Jerusalem, in its midst. All those redeemed from Old Earth have been placed in exalted positions of trust and honor, reigning as rulers and priests with the Godhead, unbelievable as it may seem after their sinful past (see Daniel 7:27; Revelation 1:6; 5:10; 20:6.) You and I have positions exactly suited to our gifts and talents and training, especially that which we received on Old Earth.

We have spent this million years growing and learning and doing ever new and greater things as God opens them up for us. We travel all over God's creation, and everywhere we go, unfallen beings never tire of hearing stories of how God is so good and so powerful that He actually saved us from what, to them, is the incomprehensible and horrifying mystery of sin.

Knowing what we now know of God's goodness and of the blessedness of complete obedience, we, too, find it hard to believe how sinful we once were. But we do not forget. The pain and sorrow are taken from us; the details do not come to mind, swallowed up as they are by the inexpressible goodness of God. But not one of us ever loses sight of just why we are here or ever finishes praising Him for it.

One day you are resting in your garden, just enjoying its peaceful, brilliant beauty, when an angel messenger appears at your side.

"Come quickly. The Father calls you."

You rise immediately and go to the Throne Room of New Jerusalem. God the Father is there with an unusual look of concern on His face. "I have an important job for you. On a certain planet, there is a child of Mine who has doubts about My will." You look shocked, and He continues, "She has not sinned. She is merely questioning. Her world was created since the end of the Age of Darkness, and she wonders whether the rule that disobedience leads to death is an arbitrary judgment of Mine. I have called for you because you and she are kindred spirits. You would be the best one to explain the truth to her in a way she would understand. Go quickly."

You go. What will you tell that sister of yours? (If you are a man, you may feel more comfortable imagining a questioning brother.) Think about it. Spend some time on it. Why should she obey, even in small, apparently unimportant particulars, such as not touching a certain tree?

Do you think, after you have told that friend all you know of good and evil (the serpent in the Garden told a half-truth, after all!), after you have opened to her the evil of evil and what it cost the Son of God to save you from it, that she can possibly consider letting her questions go on to rebellion and become sin?

I hardly think so.

Here is a suggestion. Write down your argument. Write everything you would say to a questioning brother or sister in a new garden somewhere in time and space. Make it as convincing as possible. Then, the next time you wonder about a seemingly unimportant piece of obedience, read it. And pray for the Spirit to hold you fast. He can do it. (You may also find yourself adapting what you write, as years pass and you learn more.)

There is only one way that you and I can make it to those exalted positions where we are the ones with the answers instead of the ones who are questioning—only one way to live someday in the unutterable joy of Jesus' physical presence. That is to learn now to live in the joy and peace of His spiritual presence.

Meditation is the way I practice that presence. I urge you to find the way that is best for you and begin to practice it today. You don't have to take the initiative. He has already found you or you would not be reading about spiritual things.

He is knocking. Will you open the door? The arms of a Friend await you.

" 'He will exult over you with joy, . . . He will rejoice over you with shouts of joy' " (Zephaniah 3:17). "*As* the bridegroom rejoices over the bride, so your God will rejoice over you" (Isaiah 62:5).

Meditate on that scene sometime!

If you enjoyed this book, you'll enjoy these as well:

God Said, "I Promise"

Debbonnaire Kovacs. The Ten Commandments are more than a list of DON'Ts. Debbonnaire Kovacs shows us how to look at God's law in a whole new way—as promises of things the Lord is already doing in our hearts and lives! For personal, or small-group study. [Discussion questions included!]
0-8163-1779-8. US$8.99, Can$13.49.

Escape to God

Jim Hohnberger with Tim and Julie Canuteson. The true story of how a prosperous Adventist family left everything behind to live in the wilderness and find genuine spirituality and the simple life.
0-8163-1805-0. US$13.99, Can$20.99.

The Cure for Soul Fatigue

Karl Haffner. With lots of laugh therapy along the way, and mega-doses of wisdom, Pastor Karl exposes the root causes of soul fatigue and prescribes the biblical cures to remedy them. Learn how to win over worry. Banish the blues. Get your priorities in order. Deal with discouragement. Find forgiveness. Follow your life calling, and more.
0-8163-1840-9. US$10.99, Cdn$16.49.

Order from your ABC by calling **1-800-765-6955**, or get online and shop our virtual store at **<www.adventistbookcenter.com>**.
•Read a chapter from your favorite book
•Order online
•Sign up for email notices on new products

Prices subject to change without notice.

F.C.